HEALING
FROM
HEAVEN

VOL 2

CHRIS OYAKHILOME, PhD

LoveWorld Publishing Ministry

Healing From Heaven
Vol 2

ISBN 978-37061-6-0

UNITED KINGDOM:
Christ Embassy Int'l Office
LoveWorld Conference Centre
Cheriton High Street,
Folkestone, Kent CT19 4QS
Tel:+44(0)1303 270970
Fax: 01303 274 372

USA:
Christ Embassy International USA
200 E Arrowhead Drive
Suite W-3
Charlotte, NC 28213
Tel: 972-255-1787, 704-780-4970

CANADA:
Christ Embassy Internayional Office, Canada
50 Weybright Court, Unit 43B
Toronto, ON M1S 5A8
Tel: +1 647-341-9091

NIGERIA:
LoveWorld Conference Centre
51 - 53 Kudirat Abiola Way,
Oregun, Lagos.
P.O. Box 13563 Ikeja, Lagos.
Tel:+234-8023324188,
+234-8052464131, +234-1-8925724

e-mail:cec@christembassy.org
websites: www.enterthehealingschool.org
www.christembassy.org

Contents

INTRODUCTION

Miracles are real! Irrefutable testimonies abound of God's saving power in the lives of those who come to Him in faith. The awesome miracles recorded for us in the Bible and the supernatural works of the Holy Spirit in our day bear testimony to this truth.

Many times when people find themselves in difficult situations, they turn everywhere else except to God, to alleviate the pain, the crisis or the difficulty in which they've found themselves. Yet, in Christ Jesus, God has done everything that needs to be done to guarantee a life of constant peace, victory and prosperity.

The Bible says, *"For this purpose the Son of God was manifested, that he might destroy the works of the devil" (John 10:10).* Jesus came, died, was buried and rose again to give us life and to make it possible for us to live victoriously.

Isaiah 53:5 says,

"But he was wounded for our transgressions, he was bruised for our iniquities: the chastisement of our peace was upon him; and with his stripes we are healed."

Jesus bore your infirmities and sicknesses on His own body that you may live in divine health; He took your pains that you may enjoy life to the full; He was wounded that your body may never be broken or destroyed by any infirmity. This is actually what the gospel is all about; it's the good news of Christ's salvation.

You may be reading this book today and you're wondering if there can ever be a change in your condition. The infirmity may have been there for so long, and you're wondering how this could possibly happen. But that's exactly what God specializes in doing—turning hopeless situations around! So, cheer up! There's hope for you in Christ, and you can trust Him today for a miracle!

In this second volume of Healing from Heaven, you would read extraordinary testimonies of everyday men and women who dared to believe God for a miracle. You'll meet Gugulethu Mabele, a young man who was paralyzed due to a gunshot, but was miraculously healed by the power of God! You'll read of the miraculous healing and transformation of Lorenz Marinescu, who was deaf in his left ear for twenty- seven years! You'll also encounter Daniella du Toit, who gave birth to a baby despite several doctors' predictions to the contrary! In the darkest moments of their lives when all seemed lost, they experienced the miraculous!

As you read their extraordinary testimonies, you'll discover the possibilities of faith and the reality of the power of the Holy Ghost. Be stirred in your spirit and encouraged as you see the demonstration of God's love.

This book also contains rich and inspiring teaching articles from God's Word that are sure to strengthen and build your faith in God. They'll bring fresh revelations to your spirit and prepare you to receive your miracle.

As you read, find the Healer within the pages, and locate yourself in His Word. As He did for those in this book and many others around the world who believed in Him for a miracle, He would do for you. The Bible says Jesus Christ is the same yesterday, today and forever (Hebrews 13:8). What He does for one, He would do for another under the same circumstances, because He shows no partiality! (Acts 10:34)

God's Word stands sure: He has brought healing from heaven to the world, and it's available for anyone who would believe!

Confession:

I refuse to be moved by the circumstances in my body! My faith is the victory that overcomes the world! Therefore, I declare that my faith is alive and producing results in and for me! I do not stagger at the Word of God through unbelief, but I am strong in faith and I give God the glory!

JESUS MAKES YOU WELL!

1

"And it came to pass, as Peter passed throughout all quarters, he came down also to the saints which dwelt at Lydda. And there he found a certain man named Aeneas, which had kept his bed eight years, and was sick of the palsy. And Peter said unto him, Aeneas, Jesus Christ maketh thee whole: arise, and make thy bed. And he arose immediately" (Acts 9:32-34).

In this account, the Bible tells us of a man named Aeneas and his extraordinary encounter with the Apostle Peter. Obviously, the man was a Christian, because the Bible tells us that Peter found him while he was visiting the saints at Lydda (Acts 9:32). But Aeneas was sick and paralyzed; he had been bedridden for eight long years. It was in that condition he received Christ, but he remained paralyzed.

The Bible records that one day, Peter went to that region, and thank God, he went to the very house where Aeneas was. When Peter saw him, he declared to him, "Aeneas, Jesus Christ makes you well! Get up and make your bed!" Peter was actually saying, "If you have Jesus, He makes you well. Get up and dress your bed!" No one had preached that part of the gospel to Aeneas before, and the Bible says he jumped out of his bed immediately!

Now, what was different in the message Peter preached to this man? Peter had an understanding of the gospel that is very vital. He understood that Christ lived in the man, and so he had no business being sick. This is the understanding that you should have also.

HEALING IS YOURS!

It's easy for many to accept that when a man confesses the Lord Jesus and believes that God raised Him from the dead, he is saved. But they find it difficult to accept that by the same token, that man is delivered from sickness. If the salvation of your spirit is that simple, why do you expect healing for your physical body to be complicated?

Jesus bore your sins as well as your sickness in the same sacrifice. 1 Peter 2:24 says, ***"Who his own self bare our sins in his own body on the tree, that we, being dead to sins, should live unto righteousness: by whose stripes ye were healed."*** All you have to do is to accept it and walk in the light of it.

I once heard the story of a young girl who was dying and whom the doctors had given a few days to live. She was connected to an oxygen tank, was completely bedridden, and couldn't eat any normal food. She could only take fluids. Sometime during this period, her mother, who had been taking care of her, gave her a Bible to study as she prepared to die.

One day, while the girl was reading her Bible, she came across 1 Peter 2:21-23:*"For even hereunto were ye called: because Christ also suffered for us, leaving us an example, that ye should follow his steps: who did no sin, neither was guile found in his mouth: who, when he was reviled, reviled not again; when he suffered, he threatened not; but committed himself to him that judgeth righteously: Who his own self bare our sins in his own body on the tree..."*

When she read this, she started sobbing and prayed, *"Dear Lord Jesus, thank you for taking my sins away. In a few days, I will be coming to heaven. I am so grateful that you saved my soul."*

Then, she wiped the tears from her eyes and continued reading from where she left off: **"...that we, being dead to sins, should live unto righteousness: by whose stripes ye were healed" (1 Peter 2: 24)** *"By whose stripes I was healed?!" I didn't know this before!"* she exclaimed.

Immediately, she changed her prayer and said, *"Lord Jesus, I thank you for bearing my sin. But I see here that you also took my sickness. I didn't know I was healed. Lord, I'm sorry I'm not coming home so soon!"* Then she removed the tubes connecting her to the oxygen tank, got out of bed, walked around, and shouted for her mother to come.

"*What is it honey?*" her mother asked as she came running downstairs.

"*Mama, please get me breakfast!*" the girl said excitedly.

"*You haven't taken any solid food for months; get back in bed!*" her mother chided.

"*But the Bible says I was healed by the stripes of Jesus!*" came her adamant reply.

Now her mother started crying, because she remembered the doctor had warned her that her daughter would lose her mind just before she died. Quickly, she carried her back to her bed and called the doctor. "*Doctor, hurry, my daughter is dying!*" she cried frantically.

While she was on the phone, her daughter had gotten out of bed again. This time she went into the kitchen, fixed herself a meal and started eating. When her mother saw this, she almost passed out.

Soon after, the doctor came in and she told him, "*My daughter's gone mad. She's eating solid food, which she hasn't had for months.*"

"*But I just read from the Bible that I was healed by the stripes of Jesus!*" the girl insisted.

She had had a terrible lung condition that had ruptured her lungs, and the doctor knew it was practically impossible for her to breathe without the oxygen tank. He immediately laid her back in bed and ran several checks, after which he discovered two brand new lungs in her body!

This young girl who had been given up to die would later grow up to get married and have four kids of her own, Hallelujah! Her knowledge and understanding of God's Word changed everything. The moment she got to know what Christ had done for her, she simply accepted it, acted on it and was healed instantly!

It's Beyond The Senses!

"When I see it, I'll believe it." That's some people's philosophy. But the truth is, you'll never believe that way because you're not going to see it until you first believe. Believing comes ahead of seeing.

After the resurrection of Jesus, He appeared to some of His disciples. But when they told Thomas, who wasn't there at the time, he said, ***"...Except I shall see in his hands the print of the nails, and put my finger into the print of the nails, and thrust my hand into his side, I will not believe" (John 20:25).*** That's the way some folks are. They always think others are trying to play on their intelligence, and that's sad. But like Jesus said to Timothy, I say to them: ***"...blessed are they that have not seen, and yet have believed" (John 20:29).***

How many times did you go to an airline's office to ask for their pilot's qualifying certificate before flying in their airplane? You simply got in the plane and fastened your seat belt, believing everything was all right. Or how many times did you ask the hospital board for the surgeon's qualifying certificate before going through a surgery? You simply gave yourself over to the surgeon and trusted him to do a good job.

Now, if you can believe human beings like that, how much more should you believe the time-tested and proven Word of God, which has never failed?

Receiving divine healing works the same as receiving salvation. You may not feel any different, but you know you're saved because your faith is based on the Word of God, which says, ***"if thou shalt confess with thy mouth the Lord Jesus, and shalt believe in thine heart that God hath raised him from the dead, thou shalt be saved"*** ***(Romans 10:9).***

In the same way, settle it in your heart for all time that Jesus paid for it all when He died for you on the Cross. The Bible says, ***"But he was wounded for our transgressions, he was bruised for our iniquities: the chastisement of our peace was upon him; and with his stripes we are healed"*** ***(Isaiah 53:5).***

When sickness or infirmity tries to bring you down, insist on the reality of God's Word and say, *"No, I refuse to be sick! Because Christ lives in me, He makes me well!"*

Confession:

Christ lives in me; therefore, no sickness or infirmity can dwell in my members. Jesus bore my infirmities on His body, that I may never bear any infirmity in my body. I declare today that my body is strong and healthy! Sickness and infirmity have no place in me; the life of Christ is at work in every fibre of my being, in every bone of my body and in every cell of my blood, in Jesus' mighty Name. Amen!

· -》》》 · 《《《- ·

FAITH IS THE VICTORY!

2

GUGULETHU MABELE

*H*is eyes were wide open and he could see and hear everything, but they spoke about him as though he wasn't there. He listened as his mother pleaded with the doctors to let him stay a while longer. He also heard them explain to her that it was no use. They had done all they could; it was a hopeless case. Unable to move or utter a word, he finally caught his mother's attention with his eyes. Then with his alphabet board, he communicated that he wanted to go home.

A few months earlier, twenty-two

year old Gugulethu Mabele had woken up to a life far different from what he'd always known. The last thing he remembered was partying with some friends. The next thing he knew, he was lying in a hospital bed unable to move or even speak. He felt alert in his mind, but no matter how hard he tried, he could not lift any part of his body or open his mouth to form any word. He would later learn he'd been shot in the head, and had been in a coma for several weeks.

Gugu underwent a battery of examinations as his doctors tried to deal with the complications caused by the injury to his head. *"They brought in different speech therapists, physiotherapists and psychiatrists. They also sent me for numerous brain scans,"* Gugu recalled.

The results showed that Gugu had lost crucial brain tissue resulting in the loss of all his motor functions and speech. The damage to his brain from the gunshot wound had paralyzed him from neck down. There was nothing the doctors could do.

During the next three months on admission, the young man experienced the darkest moments of his life. He was written off by the doctors as a hopeless invalid, and they made it clear that he'd never recover. *"I could tell from the statements the doctors made amongst each other whenever they came to check on me, that they had diagnosed my case as incurable. They even debated amongst one another what type of care facility would best suit my situation with my mother's medical-aid,"* Gugu said.

Gugu developed terrible bed sores as a result of the long hours he spent lying motionless in bed. *"Due to insufficient number of nurses at the hospital to attend to every patient, I developed bedsores on my right and left thighs, and on my back, which grew deeper as the days went by,"* he says.

Eventually, the doctors notified his mother of their intention to discharge him. By this time, through physiotherapy, Gugu had developed slight movement in his right hand, which allowed him to use a small alphabet board to communicate. Having done the best they could, the doctors told her that her son would never be able to walk or talk again, and he would require constant care and support for the rest of his life. *"The closest you can give him of a normal life is to get a specialized wheelchair and put him in an institution that would attend specially to his needs,"* they concluded.

Gugu's mother felt distressed as she pondered her options. *"When the hospital gave my mother the report that I would never be able to walk or talk again, and recommended the special equipment and institution that I would require for the rest of my life, she was distraught. Then, she tried to convince them to let me stay at the ward a little longer,"* he recalled.

Sensing her despair, the doctors told her the alternative would be for her to hire a nurse to care for him twenty-four hours every day, but the cost was prohibitive. Gugu's mother was not sure if taking him home would be best for him. *"My mother was hesitant about taking me home. But with the help of my alphabet board, I requested that she take me home. I knew I would die if I remained in the hospital."* With medications to help with the bedsores, Gugu left the hospital that day with his mother.

It was not until Gugu got home that he fully comprehended the gravity of his condition. He literally couldn't do anything unaided; he depended on his family members to help him do everything. *"I couldn't do all the things normal people do and take for granted. Eating independently, talking to my sister or friends, bathing, using the toilet, walking and running to the shops, cycling, playing football, or turning the page of a book were impossible. I was deprived of basically everything, except my life"* recounted Gugu.

To make matters worse, Gugu couldn't call out to get the attention of someone when he was alone, so he would ring a bell anytime he wanted help. Gugu was deeply moved by how his family members adjusted their personal lives to care for him. *"My family had to amend their ways to suit my needs, for which I will eternally be grateful. Because of me, my mother worked for only three hours every day; and when she was at work, my cousin, Vusi, bathed me, changed my catheter, and gave me my pills."*

Gugu's education at the Information Technology Department of the University of South Africa was completely discarded. His mother had been a Christian and she believed her son would one day walk and talk again by the power of God. So when she heard of the healing ministry of Pastor Chris at the Healing School, she decided to take Gugu there, with faith for a miracle. *"I'm grateful for the decision my mother took to bring me to the Healing School. I believe it saved my life,"*

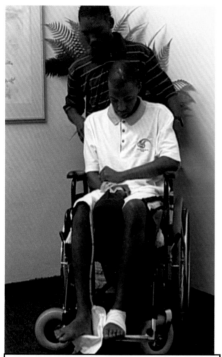

Gugu arrived the Healing School in a wheel chair, completely incapacitated

Gugu said.

Gugu was brought to the Healing School by his mother, accompanied by his cousin, Vusi. He was initially doubtful of the power of God at work in the Healing School. However, it didn't take long for that same power to transform his life! *"My mother took it upon herself to bring me to the Healing School every day without fail. At first, I was skeptical of the entire proceedings, but I was soon converted."*

As Gugu learned the Word of God at the Healing School, he observed to his amazement, that changes were beginning to take place in his life. *"After a few days of listening to the Word of God at the Healing School, I found myself eager to hear more and take seriously the things I was being taught. That was when miracles started occurring!"*

Gugu was at home one evening, watching a programme with his family, when he suddenly burst into laughter! He hadn't made a sound in more than four months! *"There was a deafening silence in the whole house,"* Gugu remembered. *"They were momentarily dumbfounded. Then, suddenly, realizing what had happened, they all began to rejoice and praise God! Thereafter, it was miracle after miracle! Gradually, I began to*

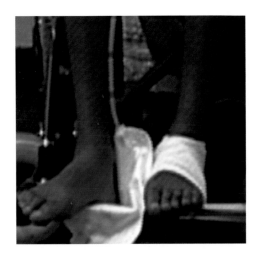

speak, use my hands, and the bed sores got healed!"

The day of the healing service is one that Gugu would always remember. *"I was expectant and excited by the ambience of faith. When others came up to testify of their miracles, I was excited because I had learnt that God is no respecter of persons; what he does for one, He'd surely do for another. So I just knew that at the end of it all I would be free from the clutches of sin and death for good."*

A few moments later, the man of God, Pastor Chris, entered the hall and began to minister the healing anointing to all who were on the healing line. *"I will never forget the day Pastor Chris ministered to me. His eyes glowed, and when I looked into them, a strong, mighty wind sent shivers through my body. And the moment he laid his hands on me,*

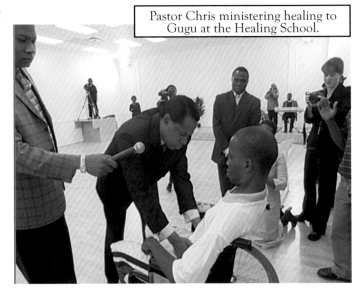

Pastor Chris ministering healing to Gugu at the Healing School.

I knew I had been healed and would never be the same again!"

Right afterwards Gugu stood up and walked for the first time since the gunshot several months before. *"It felt like I was in a dream! Indeed, it was not until the next day that I fully realized that I had been impacted by the power of God through the man of God, Pastor Chris!"*

Everything changed for Gugu from that day onward. Daily, he experienced miracles in his body, and within a short while, there was no trace of any previous abnormality! Gugu walked, talked and did everything he couldn't do previously!

He's up and walking, healed by the power of God!

"I could sit up on the couch, prepare my own meals, bathe myself, exercise my hands and feet, and go for walks around the yard as my lower body regained strength! Everyone who saw me began to say how they too needed God in their lives. Some others praised God for the transformation they witnessed in me."

Most important for Gugu was the transformation that took place in his life. *"Above all the other miraculous things that took place at the time, the best thing was what happened on my inside. I had a hunger and thirst for God's Word that nothing else could satisfy. I also grew to know and love God."*

Meeting up with Gugu five years later, he's still filled with praise and thanksgiving to God for the mighty and awesome miracle God wrought in his life through Pastor Chris. Testifying with great confidence and joy, he said, *"I am a walking miracle! The doctors said I would always have to rely on others for assistance, but today I do everything independently! I can walk, bathe myself, brush my own teeth, control my bowel movement, and drive myself anywhere I want to go! Sometimes, I just shout "Hallelujah!" as a testimony of the Lord healing my speech! I have also registered at the University of South Africa to complete my diploma, and I use my brain daily at work to manoeuvre complicated computer applications, something the doctors thought would never be possible again!"*

GUGULETHU MABELE

Gugu works today in a government establishment. He has also resumed his studies in Information Technology at the University of South Africa. With every opportunity he testifies of how the power of God healed and transformed his life at the Healing School of Christ Embassy.

Laughter

There's a popular saying that "Laughter is the best medicine." It's a manifestation of joy; an expression of mirth. It's making sounds and movements with the face and body that show joy, amusement and contentment.

Laughter causes the release of endorphins, which are the human body's natural pain relief hormones. It relieves tension, anxiety, shame and guilt, and helps one maintain a positive attitude even in negative situations. Moreover, it is able to raise energy levels, thereby completely getting rid of depression. It helps reduce stress that comes in the course of your daily activities. It also improves your emotional and mental health, and ultimately creates a sense of well-being within you.

People laugh for various reasons, but the Word of God gives us insight into the spiritual benefits of laughter. Proverbs 17:22 says, "A merry heart doeth good like a medicine...." In other words, wonderful healing power is unleashed every time you laugh! Although laughter is a psychological response to humour, it doesn't always have to be initiated by an external influence or condition. It can spring up from inside you and burst forth on the outside.

CHRIST IN YOU

3

"Even the mystery which hath been hid from ages and from generations, but now is made manifest to his saints: To whom God would make known what is the riches of the glory of this mystery among the Gentiles; which is Christ in you, the hope of glory" (Colossians 1:26-27).

*T*he greatest thing that could ever happen to a human person is to have and know the Lord Jesus Christ. In the introductory verse above, the Bible reveals the mystery that had been hid for ages and generations past but has now been manifested: "Christ in you, the hope of glory."

In Scripture, the name "Christ" is sometimes used to refer to the person of Jesus, while in other instances, it means the Church, which is His body. However, in its simple definition, "Christ" refers to the anointed One and His anointing.

It's important to understand this because the man Jesus doesn't live in you. It's only acceptable in generic terminology to say Jesus lives in you. In reality, Jesus ascended to heaven and is seated at the right hand of the Father (Ephesians 1:20). It's the Holy Spirit who brings His presence and makes His anointing known and available to God's people today (John 14:16-18).

So when the Bible says Christ is in you, it means the totality of the character and nature of the Lord Jesus and all that His anointing represents is in you. In other words, all of His life, and the power and glory of His anointing reside in you. And that, the Bible says, is "the hope of glory!"

YOUR HOPE FOR THE GLORIOUS LIFE!

Christ in you is your hope for a life of glory. If you're sick in your body today, what you need is the manifestation of Christ in your body. When Christ is manifested, everything that's not of God will leave.

This understanding is important because when a man is born again, he is recreated in his human spirit. The life of God supplants the human life with which he was born, and he becomes a new man. However, his soul, which is the seat of his emotions, will and thoughts, remains the same; that's why a person could be born again and still have the wrong thoughts in his mind. But when Christ is manifested in your soul, you would think the thoughts of God and do His will

(Romans 12:2).

Just as your mind is not instantly transformed at the new mind, your body also doesn't change the moment you become a Christian. This is why someone could be born again and still be sick and afflicted in his body. But when Christ is manifested in your body, the necessary result would be healing and divine health.

LET CHRIST TAKE ALL OF YOU!

"Jesus answered and said unto him, If a man love me, he will keep my words: and my Father will love him, and we will come unto him, and make our abode with him" (John 14:23).

Every child of God is God's dwelling place (1 Corinthians 3:16), but Christ can only manifest Himself in the life of the one who keeps His Word. He'll manifest Himself in your soul by taking charge of your mind and giving you thoughts of God. He'll also manifest Himself in your body by showing Himself alive in your tissues and organs, giving you divine healing and health.

This is what you need in your life. Much more than the healing, you need the Healer. His divine presence vitalizes your mortal body through His Spirit that lives in you. If He is manifested in your body, no sickness or infirmity can remain!

I once heard an interesting story of a certain man who had several things going wrong in his life and had been praying to God. Finally, one day, he asked God, *"I thought when I let you into my life, these problems would cease?"* God answered him, *"I can only take as much as you give me"* and went on to reveal to him how he had given Him only one room in his big house.

In that revelation, God was in His room when the devil came into the house, fought the man and wounded him. After his ordeal, he went to God complaining, *"I brought you into my house thinking I would never have any problems again?"*

But God answered, *"You gave me only one room to stay in, and as long as this is the only room I have, the devil can come into any of the others."*

At that moment, the man decided to give God two more rooms.

Later that night, there was another battle and the devil fought and wounded the man. Furious, he asked God, *"I've given you three rooms, so why did you still let the devil in?"*

God answered, *"The devil didn't come to the rooms where I stayed."*

"Okay Lord, I give You the fourth room!" the man said.

The next night, the same thing happened, and the devil still defeated him. Now the man was mad at God. *"What else do You want me to give You? I've given You four rooms and still You allowed the devil in?"*

God said, *"The house is not mine; you gave me four rooms in your house and the devil can't come into those rooms to attack you."*

Finally, with new understanding, the man said, *"Okay Lord, please take the whole house!"*

The devil came again that night, but this time, there was a new Owner of the house! God stood right at the gate and the devil couldn't come in! The man slept so well that night, and when he woke up the next morning he said, *"Lord, I had a wonderful sleep! Did You see the devil at all?"*

God said, *"Well, he came but I stopped him at the gate, because the house is now mine!"* Hallelujah!

This is what you ought to do with your life; turn your entire being over to God. If you let Him only into your spirit, He'll be there, but you may still think the wrong thoughts and do the wrong things. You may not obey Him when He gives you certain instructions. Your body may still be bruised and afflicted. But when you give Him your whole spirit, soul and body, He'll manifest Himself in every area of your life!

Make it a priority in your life to have a rich fellowship with the Lord Jesus and exalt His Word in your life. Jesus said, **"If a man love me, he will keep my words: and my Father will love him, and we will come unto him, and make our abode with him" (John 14:23).**

What you really need is a relationship with the Healer and His manifested presence in your life. Then, you can say, "Christ lives in me now. Therefore, this pain cannot continue. Jesus is Lord over my spirit, soul, and body; disease cannot stay in me!" Praise God!

Confession:

Christ is Lord over my spirit, soul and body. Therefore, no disease or infirmity has any place in me. No weapon fashioned against me shall prosper. Jesus has all authority over my body and I declare that I dwell daily in health and strength, in the mighty Name of Jesus. Amen!

A DIVINE TRANSFORMATION

4

A wave of sadness flooded her heart as she looked at her daughter. It all seemed so unfair and cruel that the little girl should bear the brunt of the way she had lived her own life. It had been several weeks since she received the report from the doctors, yet she was still tormented by the thoughts of leaving her eight-year-old daughter orphaned.

It seemed like yesterday when Atabia Mlauzi went to

ATABIA MLAUZI

the hospital for a check-up. For several weeks she had experienced a dull nagging headache and running nose. She also found that she tired easily with very little activity. To nip the situation in the bud, Atabia took a number of self-help medications, but the symptoms continued unabated. So she decided the hospital was the place to go to find answers.

Atabia got answers from the hospital all right, but instead of providing succour, they threw her into depths of sadness she never knew existed. The tests had revealed a deadly diagnosis: she was HIV positive. That was the

Atabia's initial test result, indicating she was HIV Positive.

reason for all the symptoms she had experienced in the past weeks.

Atabia was terrified at the report because she knew that HIV was synonymous with a death sentence. Death was certain for the victim; it was only a matter of time. *"I felt terrible when I received the report that I was HIV positive. I thought that was the end of my life, because I knew that with HIV, there was no hope,"* Atabia recalled

In no uncertain terms, the doctors went ahead to explain to her what she already knew: HIV had no cure, and the available medications could only help to boost her immune system against the ravaging nature of the disease. There was nothing medically that could be proffered as a final solution.

Little in life made sense to Atabia after that day. `She was only twenty-eight years old, with a young daughter and a whole life ahead of her, but everything suddenly became meaningless. *"I felt so lost,"* she recalled. *"I felt I had lost myself."*

Within months, Atabia became a shadow of her former self. She became terribly emaciated and listless, as she gradually withdrew from life. The young lady was plagued with chronic insomnia and sinusitis which caused a discoloration of the skin beneath her eyes.

Constantly engulfed with thoughts of death, Atabia lost all hope and began to live as one who had her days numbered. *"I started living a different life; I didn't care anymore. Whenever I got money I thought I should just use it all, since I was going to die anyway. I was hopeless."*

The next two years were the most miserable for Atabia. She lived constantly in fear, not knowing if she'd survive each day. *"I actually contemplated committing suicide at a point,"* she admitted.

Sometime during this period, Atabia heard about the Healing School and the awesome miracles that took place there. *"After I started attending Christ Embassy, someone told me about the Healing School,"* she said. However, it was not until Atabia received a copy of the Healing School magazine that she realized she too could receive a miracle at the Healing School.

"I thought the Healing School was only for people in wheelchairs until I got a copy of the Healing School magazine. In it I read the story of a lady who was HIV positive and she got healed at the Healing School! I thought, 'If God could do it for her, He'd definitely do it for me.' Then I decided to attend the Healing School."

At the Healing School, Atabia was deeply impacted by the teaching of God's Word. Her heart leapt for joy and her faith was strengthened as she received God's truths on divine healing and the life of God in a believer.

Then, the moment came when the man of God, Pastor Chris would minister to Atabia. *"That remains the most beautiful experience in my life,"* she would say afterwards. The power of God that attended his entrance was overwhelming; Atabia felt a miracle take place instantly in her body! *"The*

Atabia receiving a huge dose of the healing anointing from the man of God.

moment the man of God entered the hall, I suddenly felt cool and filled with peace. I knew I had received my miracle!"

Immediately he entered the hall, Pastor Chris started to minister the healing anointing to all who were on the healing line, one after the other. A few moments later, he stood before Atabia, took hold of her hands, and blew on her. Overwhelmed by the power of God, Atabia fell straight on the floor. *"When the man of God touched me, I felt the anointing all over me and I fell down. I'm not sure of anything else that happened but when I got up, all I knew was that I had been healed!"*

It was a beautiful sight to behold Atabia rise from the floor and break into a run, in awe of the miracle she knew she had received. Tears flowed freely down her face, as she ran with her hands lifted in gratitude to God!

An exuberant Atabia, rejoicing at her healing.

A few days afterwards, it was joy unspeakable for Atabia when she returned to the hospital and was tested negative for HIV. The power of God had healed her body of a medically impossible situation, and she couldn't thank Him enough.

Several months later, a completely transformed Atabia returned to the Healing School to testify of her awesome miracle. *"I'm free, praise God!"* she said with great joy. *"Now, I can plan a future. Also, now when I see my daughter, I see a mighty woman of God! Thank you Pastor Chris for your ministry that has touched my life and is touching many lives all over the world!"*

Since then, Atabia has won many to the Lord as she shares the news of God's saving power through her testimony. She is also actively involved in her local Church.

Boosting Your Immune System

The immune system is the body's natural defence against infectious organisms. A healthy immune system protects the body against infections and diseases. There are several ways to boost your body's immune system. Outlined below are five great ways to do that naturally:

1. Watch What You Eat:

A diet rich in antioxidants is essential to supporting your immune system. Antioxidants are abundant in many fruits and vegetables. Healthy fats such as omega-3 fatty acids available in oily fish, flaxseed, and krill oil also help to increase your body's production of compounds involved in regulating immunity. Including garlic and ginger in your meals is also helpful. Garlic has been proven to possess virus-fighting and bacteria-killing properties, while ginger is a natural anti-inflammatory.

2. Drink Plenty of Water:

Drinking plenty of water and steering clear of sugary beverages, like soda and energy drinks, may also help boost your immunity by cleansing your system. Also as much as you can, avoid caffeinated drinks. Caffeine robs your body of minerals and vitamins, and dehydrates you. If you drink coffee, make sure you add an additional two glasses of water to your water intake per cup of coffee.

3. Exercise Regularly:

Regular exercise can mobilize your "T cells", a type of white blood cell known to guard the body against infection. Studies have shown that people who engage in regularly in moderate exercises (such as brisk walking) are generally healthier than those who don't.

4. Sleep Well:

The amount of sleep people need varies widely. It ranges from 5 to 10 hours per night. It is important to find your own personal sleep requirement and get it! Sleep has been linked to balanced hormone levels, clear thinking and reasoning, improved mood, and healthy skin.

5. Take Care of Yourself:

Caring for yourself and doing things that you love help immensely to boost your wellbeing. Spend time with your loved ones and engage regularly in activities that truly make you happy. You'd find that you'd live healthier and stronger!

THE OVERCOMING LIFE

5

In 1 John 4:4, the Bible says, *"Ye are of God, little children, and have overcome them: because greater is he that is in you, than he that is in the world."*

"Ye are of God...." This is John's testimony to Christians, that their origin is in God. In other words, the Christian is born of God, and therefore, has the same life and nature with God.

It's important to note that the verse doesn't say you shall overcome them; it says you have overcome them. This is not a promise; it is a statement of fact. You're not trying to overcome; you have overcome already!

Also observe it doesn't say you have overcome them "because you're strong" or "because you're very spiritual!" No! You have overcome them because the One in you is greater than the one in the world!

Colossians 1:13 says, *"Who hath delivered us from the power of*

darkness, and hath translated us into the kingdom of his dear Son:"
The natural man is under the dominion of the devil and therefore
requires deliverance. But the new creation man who has been brought
out of the dominion of the devil into the kingdom of God's dear Son
doesn't need to be delivered again.

UNDERSTAND THE OVERCOMING LIFE

When a man is born again, the life of the first Adam, which is
subject to sin and death, is supplanted by the life and nature of Christ.
This new man is reborn with a brand new life. He is a completely new
species of being that never existed before. In **2 Corinthians 5:17,** the
Bible says, **"Therefore if any man be in Christ, he is a new creature:
old things are passed away; behold, all things are become new. And
all things are of God…"**

In reality, the new creature has his origin in God. His life comes
from God, and this life can never be defeated, destroyed or brought
down. That's what the Bible actually means in 1 John 4:4 where it says,
**"Ye are of God, little children, and have overcome them: because
greater is he that is in you, than he that is in the world."**

FUNCTION IN GOD'S REALM!

*"And these signs shall follow them that believe; In my name
shall they cast out devils; they shall speak with new tongues;*

They shall take up serpents; and if they drink any deadly thing, it shall not hurt them; they shall lay hands on the sick, and they shall recover" (Mark 16:17-18).

It's important to note that this is not a promise but a statement of fact unveiling your true description. In other words, by virtue of your new birth, you're no longer subject to diseases and infections. You now have within you the overcoming life of God, and that life cannot be brought down by any infirmity.

Back in the Old Testament, God told the children of Israel, *"... the life of the flesh is in the blood..." (Leviticus 17:11).* Their lives were dependent on the blood running through their veins. However, the moment you're born again, your life no longer comes from your blood but from God and His Spirit dwelling in you. **John 1:12** says, *"But as many as received him, to them gave he power to become the sons of God, even to them that believe on his name:"* Romans 8:11 also declares, *"But if the Spirit of him that raised up Jesus from the dead dwell in you, he that raised up Christ from the dead shall also quicken your mortal bodies by his Spirit that dwelleth in you."* Therefore, live everyday in the reality of who you are. You're no longer what you used to be. The life of God within you is greater than any infirmity. It is superior to the devil, demons and all manner of disease!

GO FOR THE WORD!

Hosea 4:6 says, ***"My people are destroyed for the lack of knowledge...."*** Many are oppressed and afflicted by the devil because they lack the knowledge of God's Word. This is the reason you must take your study of God's Word seriously. It will show you who you really are and what belongs to you in Christ Jesus.

The truth is, the more of God's Word you receive into your spirit, the greater insight you'll have into the life of God in you and consequently function in. That life will become so real to you and it'll be impossible for sickness to dominate you.

Make up your mind not to have a casual relationship with God's Word. Go after it like you would go after a treasure; it will transform your life and cause you to walk in the reality of eternal life!

Confession:

I am born of God; my origin is in Him! No sickness has the power or ability to destroy my body! I have the overcoming life of God in me, and that makes me indestructible and impregnable to disease and infirmity, Hallelujah!

One Moment With God!

6

IYOBO ODIASE

The day began like any other day, only this time he woke up with a strange weakness in his body and a throbbing pain in his head. A normally energetic young man, twenty-four-year-old Iyobo Odiase found it unusual. Immediately presuming it was due to insufficient rest, Iyobo muscled himself out of bed and got ready for work.

A workman in a large manufacturing company, Iyobo struggled to discharge his responsibilities that day, as the weakness and headaches remained with him. The young man was feverish and his body felt sore with pain. Refusing to go down with the pain and weakness he felt, Iyobo strove to complete his tasks for the day. Once done, he headed straight home, convinced that some extra hours of sleep was all he needed.

Any hopes Iyobo had of feeling better the next morning quickly dissipated when he woke up feeling worse than ever. Presuming this time that he had come down with a bout of fever, he decided to take some medication to contain it. However, when Iyobo got to work that day, his experience was the same as the day before. He felt drained of energy and his body ached with pain.

The day after, Iyobo became agitated when he found that not only did he feel weak and suffer excruciating body aches, he could not pass out urine from his body. At that point no one needed to tell him something was seriously amiss and he needed urgent medical attention.

At the hospital, he received a most unusual diagnosis. Tests revealed that he was suffering from nephrotic syndrome. Iyobo sat back in shock as he tried to comprehend the report. "*Nephrotic syndrome is a disorder of vital blood vessels in the kidney which is characterized by decreased production of urine, the presence of blood and protein in the urine, and oedema,*" the doctor explained.

Clarifying further, the doctor said the disorder in his kidneys was the reason for all the symptoms he had been experiencing. Fully aware of the gravity of the condition, the doctor prescribed some medications and gave him a long list of foods to avoid, hoping this help would help control the condition.

However, within just one week, life changed drastically for Iyobo. In addition to the previous symptoms, his entire body began to swell. From his head right down to his toe, Iyobo's body appeared as though it had been inflated with air. He lost appetite for food, and his stomach protruded grotesquely with the smallest meal. He later found that it was due to the retention of fluid in his body, as he could not pass out waste normally.

More distressing for Iyobo was the fact that the swelling occurred most severely at night while he slept. Consequently, every night Iyobo was scared to sleep because he knew the next morning he would be visibly altered with swollen eyes and a puffy face.

During the day, the swelling moved to his legs and feet, and at such times he found it difficult to walk or bend. As a result, Iyobo had to resort to lying down constantly to reduce the swelling and ease the pains.

Returning to the hospital for help, Iyobo was distraught when the doctors told him he'd have to have an urgent kidney dialysis, to remove the dangerous waste products from his body. This was however, not a cure. Being a treatment that required a lump sum which Iyobo couldn't afford at the time, he returned home that day dejected and concerned for his life.

Within a few days, Iyobo began to feel intense pains in his throat, eyes and mouth. He felt excruciating pains in his ribs and abdomen whenever he attempted to speak. He took the doctors' prescriptions as best he could, but without the dialysis, his health only worsened.

At this point, Iyobo decided to try traditional treatments, on the advice of a friend, but the results were no different. Some colleagues and people in his neighbourhood began to avoid him, seeing that death loomed over him. On several occasions, Iyobo wept as he wondered if he'd ever be free to live again.

For the next two months, every day for Iyobo was a battle for his life. A young man who was so full of life and energy suddenly found himself on the precipice of death.

Rays of hope shone in Iyobo's heart when a family member told him about the healing ministry of Pastor Chris, and the demonstration of the power of God at the Healing School. It was a long five-hour journey by road from his home in Benin City, but Iyobo decided to head to the Healing School in Lagos, with faith for a miracle.

At the Healing School, Iyobo felt enveloped by the love and power of God. He was unable to walk, so he had to lie in a stretcher due to the swelling and weakness he felt all over his body, but he knew he had come to the right place.

Then his moment with God came! Pastor Chris stood before him and laid his hands on his chest. With eyes filled with compassion,

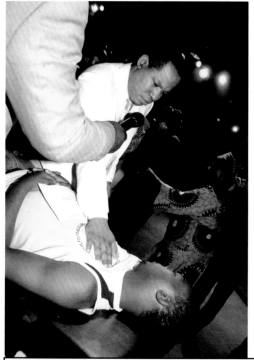

Pastor Chris transferring healing power into Iyobo's body

the man of God took a hold of his hand and motioned him to rise. Instantly, Iyobo rose to his feet and stood! Then, with his gaze intently fixed on Iyobo, the man of God sharply rebuked the evil spirits that had caused the condition and ordered them to come out of him.

At that moment, tears began to flow freely from Iyobo's eyes. But God still had some more for him! The man of God instructed him to inhale the anointing radiating from his hands. He then laid his hands on his chest, perfecting his healing. Recalling this experience, Iyobo says, "*I didn't have any strength, but when the man of God told me to breathe in and out, strength came into me instantly! And when he laid his hands on my chest; I fell down and started shivering. While on the floor, I felt something come out of me, and then something come into me. I just knew it was the power of God, and immediately I stood up!"*

Recognizing that a miracle had definitely taken place in his life, Iyobo jumped and ran around with joy. A few moments before this, he couldn't stand or walk, but here he was praising God with gusto! *"I'm grateful to God Almighty for what He's done for me. He's done*

"Praise God, I'm healed!"

what doctors and traditional medicine couldn't do!" And yet there was more in store as Iyobo would experience more miracles in his body when he returned home. *"Two days after I left the Healing School, I started passing out urine normally and I could eat well! All the swelling gradually reduced, and I could do everything that I couldn't do before!"*

Six months later, sitting before an excited congregation at the Healing School, Iyobo testified of his awesome miracle and the transformation that had taken place in his life. The changes that had taken place in his body were simply divine! His body had been restored to its normal size and he shone with a radiance that a man could only receive after an encounter with the Lord!

"I'm a living testimony!" he exulted. *"Some people said I wouldn't survive it, but here I am today, a living testimony of the power of God! When I sleep now, I wake up normally! My eyes don't swell anymore, and I can do everything that I couldn't do before! I'm alive again, praise God!"*

It's been three years since Iyobo was healed by the power of God at the Healing School, and every day he wakes up thankful to God for touching his life and making him free to live again.

"Look at me now!" A transformed Iyobo is the picture of perfect health.

Eat Healthy: Eat Vegetables!

Vegetables are some of the most natural foods in the world. They contain vitamins, minerals and thousands of other plant chemicals known to provide health benefits. Vegetables are low in fat and calories; a good source of dietary fibre that also provide us with extra energy. All these help to control weight effectively, as they fill the stomach faster and limit the total amount of food consumed.

The presence of many vitamins and other chemicals in vegetables supply the body with nutrients necessary to boost energy production within the muscle cells. This gives a natural feeling of vitality and the energy to become more active.

Vegetables are also low in sodium, so they help reduce water gain. Sodium is present in virtually all processed foods; it causes the body to hold water within the interstitial areas of the body. It's been estimated that many average people may be holding up to five pounds of additional water caused from a high intake of sodium. Any reduction in sodium will help lose water weight and if we eat more vegetables, our sodium intake naturally lowers.

So, make a healthy choice and eat vegetables today. They may not look too attractive , but they've got immense benefits!

POWER FOR CHANGE

7

"But ye shall receive power, after that the Holy Ghost is come upon you: and ye shall be witnesses unto me both in Jerusalem, and in all Judaea, and in Samaria, and unto the uttermost part of the earth" (Acts 1:8).

One of the biggest things Christ brought to us is the possibility to receive the Holy Spirit. When the Holy Spirit takes residence in a believer, He changes everything. If a man were weak and timid, he'd immediately receive strength and boldness. If he were sick and infirm, his body would be vitalized. If he were in the dark about a particular situation, he'd receive the guidance that he required. There's absolutely nothing in the world compared to the presence of the Holy Spirit in a child of God!

YOU CAN EFFECT CHANGES!

In **Acts 1:8,** the Bible says, **"...ye shall receive power after that the Holy Ghost is come upon you...."** The moment you received the

Holy Spirit, you received the power of God into your life.

Now, the word translated "power" is from the Greek word "Dunamis," which means the dynamic ability to cause changes. It's from this word that we get the English word "dynamo," an inherent power generator.

Jesus never exaggerated! When He spoke, He spoke absolute truth. When He said, *"...ye shall receive power after that the Holy Ghost is come upon you,"* He meant exactly what He said. He carefully chose the expression to communicate the quality and potency of the power that we would have.

After the Holy Ghost came to live within you, you received inherent power. This power resides in you and functions independently of any other power. With this power of the Holy Ghost in you, you don't need to call for power from above. You have inherent power within you to effect any change you desire. This means you can actually effect changes in your body.

It isn't God's desire and purpose for you to be a victim of sickness, disease or infirmity. In **Romans 8:37**, the Bible says, ***"Nay, in all these things we are more than conquerors through him that loved us."***

However, many Christians live as victims and suffer infirmities in their bodies. But that's not the life Jesus brought. Jesus said, *"...ye shall receive power, after that the Holy Ghost is come upon you..."* (Acts 1:8). Simple truth, but when you accept and understand it, your life will be changed forever!

ACTIVATING THE POWER!

Some Christians haven't learnt how to put the power of the Holy Ghost in them to work, so they're constantly looking for help and seeking someone to pray for them. It's important to understand that if the Holy Spirit lives within you, you don't need any other outside power; He is the power-giver! Therefore, you should never live as a victim of sickness, because you have all that you require within you to change any condition in your body!

Speaking in tongues is one sure way to activate the power of the Holy Ghost in you. The Bible says, ***"...he that speaketh in an unknown tongue speaketh not unto men, but unto God: for no man understandeth him; howbeit in the spirit he speaketh mysteries" (1 Corinthians 14:2).*** Through speaking in tongues, we communicate with God and speak forth mysteries or secret truths.

Some Christians don't believe in speaking in other tongues, and that's the reason they have many conflicts in their lives. They don't know it, but that's where the power is. In **1 Corinthians 14:4**, the Bible says, ***"He that speaketh in an unknown tongue edifieth himself...."*** The word "edifieth" there means "to embolden" or "to charge up" as you would a battery.

If you were weak and felt overwhelmed by a condition in your body, spend quality time speaking in other tongues. It won't be long before the power of God will rise within you and prevail over that condition.

Understand that the power of the Holy Ghost in you is greater than anything in this world (1 John 4:4). When His power is at work in you, no infirmity can stand against you successfully. You may have been born with a deformed heart; it doesn't matter anymore; you don't have to suffer any more crises. Now that you have the Holy Ghost residing in you, you can cause a change! Speak in other tongues and activate the power of the Spirit. Be edified through the Spirit and see the change you desire come to pass.

Confession:

The Holy Ghost lives in me, therefore, I have the dynamic ability to effect changes! I refuse to permit anything contrary to God's Word in my body. As I speak in other tongues, I declare that supernatural changes are taking place in me, in Jesus' Name. Amen!

A New Day For Sandra

8

With careful and calculated steps she walked into the Church hall. Once inside, her eyes quickly panned the pews directly facing the platform. A wave of relief swept through her when she saw that her seat had not yet been filled. Then, with some effort to keep her neck straight, she walked to the seat and joined the service.

Life had not always been this way for forty-seven-year-old Sandra Fernandez. It was in 1998 when she first felt some pain in her neck. Back then, they were slight spasms

SANDRA FERNANDEZ

that coursed through her neck occasionally, but they always left as quickly as they came. *"It wasn't so bad at the time, so I continued with it,"* Sandra recalled.

An energetic and assiduous homemaker, Sandra carried on with her life with hopes that the pains would fade away with time. However, the exact opposite happened. The pains came more frequently and intensely. Before long, Sandra found that she experienced severe pains whenever she attempted to turn her head sideways. She also observed that most evenings her head would pound with pain.

Within a few years, these painful experiences became constant for Sandra. *"I could no longer move my neck freely, and I would have severe headaches."* To heighten her concern, Sandra also found that her hands would occasionally become numb and unresponsive. It was at this time that she decided to go to the hospital to find out what was really happening to her.

Her doctor diagnosed her condition as cervical spondylosis, a chronic degeneration of the cervical spine. He explained that this was the reason for the increasing pains she felt in her neck and the numbness she experienced. He then prescribed some medications to relieve the pains.

Sandra took the medications prescribed to her and was glad when she felt some respite. But her joy was short-lived as the pains re-surfaced in a short while with intensity. She had another x-ray and was given more medications. *"This time, the pains didn't leave,"* she recalled.

"I could not turn my head sideways or bend my head. I would have severe pains at the back of my neck, which went down to my shoulders and hands. So, I had to keep my head straight all the time. Even in Church, I always tried to find a seat that faced the pulpit. If I sat at the side, and turned sideways, I would have pains in my head and shoulders, and the rest of the day would be difficult for me."

Sandra also found that whenever her hands were inactive for a while, her right hand would become numb. Sometimes, she would have to use her left hand to massage the right one intensely to restore feeling to it. *"I always had to use my other hand to get the right hand started,"* she remembered. More disturbing for Sandra was the fact that anytime this happened, she would feel faint and have an irritable sensation all over her face and suffer severe headaches. At such times, she would be unable to do anything effectively and would have to lie down to regain herself.

A mother who cherished the time she gave to the upkeep of her family and home, Sandra now found it difficult to perform household chores. *"I did my housework with great pain; I always had to lie down to rest at least three or four times during the day. My hobby was reading, but I couldn't do it anymore because I couldn't keep my head down for more than a few minutes."*

Desperately desirous of normalcy in her life, Sandra returned to the hospital for a solution. This was when the doctor made it clear to her that there was no remedy for her condition and that she'd have to live with the pain for the rest of her life. *"He told me there was no cure; the cartilages in my neck bones had been wasted, and at my age, they could never grow back."* To help, the doctor advised that she wear a neck brace, but Sandra recalled, *"I didn't want a neck brace, so the doctor told me I always had to keep my neck straight, and advised me to do certain neck exercises and massages."*

Much as Sandra tried to do everything her doctor said, the pains remained with her. Gradually, she became handicapped as she could not lift up her arms beyond a particular level or turn them backwards. She also found it difficult to lift anything with her right hand. Sure enough, the condition began to affect her emotionally. *"I got down emotionally because I used to be a very hardworking person, and I could no longer do all the things I wanted to. Most of the time, I had to stay in bed resting and keeping my head in one position. I also had fears that one day I might become paralyzed."*

A new day dawned for Sandra when she watched the Healing School programme on LoveWorld TV for the first time. *"When I saw the miracles and the testimonies, I thought to myself, 'If I should go there, I would be totally*

Sandra at the healing service, full of faith and expectation.

healed!'"

Propelled by her faith, in March 2008, Sandra made the twenty hour journey by air to the Healing School in Johannesburg, from her home in Sri Lanka. *"The very first day I got into the Healing School, I believed that I would have a miracle. The whole place was just as I expected!"*

Sandra's faith soared higher when she witnessed a healing service with the man of God, Pastor Chris shortly after her arrival at the Healing School. *"That was my most memorable moment at the Healing School— the first miracle meeting I attended, where I saw many incurable diseases healed by the power of God!"*

On the day the man of God ministered to Sandra, she knew she was going to have the same experience, and her faith further increased

Pastor Chris reading Sandra's case card as he prepares to minister to her.

when she listened to past students of the Healing School testify of their own miracles. *"I knew that the same would happen to me; I was expectant."*

Standing on the healing line, Sandra worshipped God with many others who also anticipated the miraculous. Just then, Pastor Chris stepped into the hall where they were. *"As he came towards me, I expected to receive my healing."* At that moment, the man of God laid his hands on her back and Sandra immediately fell under the power of God. *"When he laid his hand on me, I felt a wave of current, like an electric shock, go through my body, and then I fell down and started to vibrate all over my body. When I got up, I didn't feel the pain in my neck and the numbness in my hand anymore. I felt so great!"*

After several years of pain, Sandra was gloriously healed in a moment by the power of God, and nothing could match the joy she felt as she realized the effective power of her faith!

A few months later, Sandra returned to the Healing School to testify of her miracle and the beautiful life she now lives. *"I don't have the pains in my neck, shoulders and hands anymore!"* she said with great joy. *"Now, I can lift my hands without any problems and turn them in any direction!"* she said, demonstrating as she spoke. *"I do all my housework now without any pain; I don't rest so frequently anymore. I work from morning till evening! Also, I don't*

Sandra, completely healed

have to keep my head straight at all times anymore!"

More than the healing Sandra received at the Healing School, her life was also transformed by the power of God. *"Through the teaching of God's Word and the power of the Holy Ghost at the Healing School, my life has been changed and my faith level increased. I'm not the same person anymore. My relationship with God has also grown enormously; there are no words to explain it! Now, when I study God's Word, I practise it and put my faith to work,"* she enthused.

It's been two years since Sandra received her healing, and she has returned to the Healing School on several occasions with many others, to be impacted by the same anointing that healed her body and transformed her life forever!

Today, Sandra is actively involved in missionary work in her country. She also participates extensively in numerous evangelical activities in her local church. Through her tremendous soul winning efforts, many in her country have been won to the Lord!

A radiant Sandra testifying at the Healing School several months after her miracle.

The Importance of Recreation

Recreation can be defined as the refreshment of one's mind and body through activity that amuses or stimulates.

Research and findings have shown that recreational activities have health and mental benefits, and help in the development of the psychological and social tendencies of individuals.

Recreation could be active or passive, or a combination of the two. Passive recreation includes enjoying a song, watching a football match or reading. On the other hand, active recreation includes running, cycling or playing basketball with friends.

Active recreation, which involves more physical activity, makes an individual less prone to obesity. It is excellent for elevating the heart rate, and helps boost the immune system.

Recreation and leisure activities can help alleviate depression and increase positive moods. Rest, relaxation and revitalization through recreation are essential to managing stress in today's busy and demanding world, and provide a medium in which participants can gain personal satisfaction.

Get involved in recreational activities; the health benefits are rewarding!

THE IMPACT OF THE HOLY SPIRIT ON THE HUMAN BODY

9

The key to living a glorious and prosperous life on earth is the Holy Spirit. However, many people who have the Holy Spirit still go through a lot of things that they shouldn't. They suffer the same problems that others who don't have the Holy Spirit suffer. Then they wonder, *"What's the advantage, if the same things that happen to others who don't have the Holy Spirit happen to me?"*

The Holy Spirit has a ministry in your physical body as He does in your spirit and soul; and it's important you learn about it so you can take advantage of it in your life.

YOUR BODY IS GOD'S PROPERTY!

When you were born again, it wasn't just your spirit that became one with Christ. Your physical body also became a part of Him. In **1 Corinthians 6:15**, the Bible says, **"Know ye not that your bodies are the members of Christ?..."**

It's important to note that the Bible says "your bodies" and not "the body." This clearly shows that the Apostle Paul was referring to our individual bodies. This means that Christ functions through your body.

1 Corinthians 6:19 expresses a similar thought. It says, ***"...know ye not that your body is the temple of the Holy Ghost which is in you, which ye have of God, and ye are not your own?"*** When the Bible says here that your physical body is the temple of the Holy Spirit, and you're not your own, it shows that He's not in you by your sheer invitation; He owns you! You don't belong to yourself or even to your earthly parents; you belong to God!

God purchased you with the precious blood of Jesus Christ, and now you have the responsibility to glorify Him in your body. **1 Corinthians 6:20** says, ***"For ye are bought with a price: therefore glorify God in your body, and in your spirit, which are God's."*** You are the custodian or caretaker of your body for the Lord. You should therefore rule your body in the way that pleases Him. Let neither sin nor sickness reign in your body anymore, nor yield your body as instruments of unrighteousness unto sin; but yield your body to the Lord (Romans 6:13).

If there's anything in your body that's not from God, you ought to insist that your body comply with the Word of God and not accommodate satanic influences. Say, *"No! I refuse to be sick! My body is the temple of the Holy Ghost. Therefore, I command every cell of my body* to comply with the Word of God; I reject this growth (or pain, or infection, or infirmity). Leave my body in the Name of Jesus Christ!"

THE MINISTRY OF THE HOLY GHOST IN YOUR BODY

"And what agreement hath the temple of God with idols? For ye are the temple of the living God; as God hath said, I will dwell in them, and walk in them; and I will be their God, and they shall be my people" (2 Corinthians 6:16).

The word "walk" used in this verse of Scripture is from the Greek word "emperipateo," which literally means "to perambulate." To perambulate means to walk up and down the border of a property in a supervisory manner. It actually refers to the supervisory activity of an official who has been assigned to the border of a property. His responsibility is to renew the boundaries or see that old ones are in good condition.

Now, when God says, "I will walk in them," He's actually saying, "I will perambulate in them!" This is the ministry of the Holy Spirit in your body! He perambulates your body, thus renewing your physical members and maintaining them in the best condition.

Also in **Romans 8:11, *the Bible says, "But if the Spirit of him that raised up Jesus from the dead dwell in you, he*** *that raised up Christ from the dead shall also quicken your mortal bodies by his Spirit that dwelleth in you."*

If you study this verse of scripture properly, you would find that the word "quicken" means to "vitalize, make alive, or give life." In other words, the Holy Spirit is the One Who gives life to your body. Your body is not sustained by the blood flowing through your veins but by the power of the Holy Spirit in you.

This means that with the Holy Spirit in you, no sickness or infirmity should have the power or ability to break your body. The Holy Spirit is constantly at work in you; so your body should never be brought down by sickness or infirmity. Remember, your body is the temple of the Holy Spirit; He lives in your body. **2 Corinthians 4:16** declares, **"*...though our outward man perish, the inward man is renewed day by day."***

TAKE ADVANTAGE OF HIS MINISTRY

In Matthew 14:24-33, the Bible gives us the extraordinary account of Peter's walk on water. In the thirtieth verse, however, the Bible says, **"*But when he saw the wind boisterous, he was afraid; and beginning to sink, he cried, saying, Lord save me" (Matthew 14:30).*** Jesus immediately reached out, got hold of him, and asked, **"*...why did you doubt?" (Matthew 14:31).*** This tells us something very striking. If the Master hadn't done something to save Peter, he would have drowned right in His presence.

There are people who suffer in the presence of God. It's not enough to say, "I believe in God," or "Christ lives in me." You've got to take advantage of His presence. Act on His Word!

First, you have to recognize Him and give Him the liberty to function in your life. Understand that Christianity is not a religion. It is the living, pulsating life of God in the human body. It is God at home in a human being, divinity at work in humanity. Christianity is a real relationship between a real God and a human being, and that relationship transforms the individual into the image or representation of God (2 Corinthians 3:18). So recognize His presence in you and give Him the pre-eminence in your life.

Secondly, activate His power through your words of faith. In the account in Matthew 14:24-33, when Peter stepped out in faith, he activated the power of God and walked on the water. But when fear attacked his heart, he began to sink. Fear activates the power of darkness and failure, but faith always activates the power of God.

Speak words of faith to your body at all times; don't speak negative words of fear and unbelief. Tell yourself that the Holy Spirit is at work in you, and He gives life to your body. Therefore, no sickness can remain!

As you do this consistently with faith in your heart, you'll find that the power of God will always be activated in your life, and the ministry of the Holy Ghost in your body will become your everyday experience.

Confession:

I am the temple of the Holy Ghost and my body functions for God. Therefore, every organ, tissue and cell in my body complies with the Word of God. My body is not sustained by blood, but by the vitalizing power of the Holy Spirit in me. I declare that the Holy Spirit is at work in me; therefore, my body is daily renewed! I dwell continually in health through the working of His mighty power in me, Hallelujah!

A MIGHTY DELIVERANCE

10

*I*sn't it ironic that an entire lifetime can be altered for better or for worse in an instant? This was the case with Patience Agboghoroma when she woke up one fateful morning. Little did she know that her whole life would be knocked out of course in a moment of time by a single event.

It happened in a split second. She had just taken her bath when, somehow, as she attempted to step out of the bathtub, she slipped and hit her bathroom floor with a loud thud. Everything happened so fast

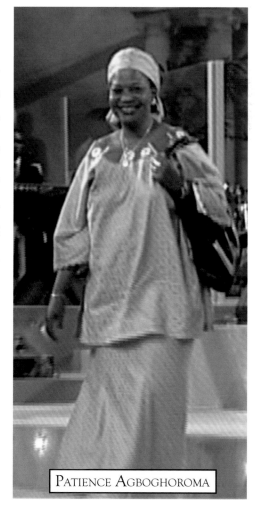

PATIENCE AGBOGHOROMA

and she couldn't prevent it.

A normally energetic and sturdy woman, she immediately tried to get up, but it was as though her whole body had been immobilized by the fall. Her legs felt stiff and her body sore with indescribable pain. *"There was no one else at home. My husband was at work and the children were not at home either,"* Patience recalled. Finally, with all the energy she could muster, she struggled to her feet and found her way to her bed, where she lay until her husband came.

When her husband returned home about an hour later, his heart sank when he saw the state she was in. She told him about the fall and the severe pains she was feeling in her back and right leg. Wasting no time, he took her to their family clinic, hoping it wasn't too serious.

At the clinic, sweet relief washed over the couple when the doctor told them nothing had gone wrong. The pains she felt were only due to the impact of the fall, and with some pain relievers she'd be fine. Patience returned home that day with her husband, thankful there was nothing more to it. Indeed, in a short while, she got better. *"The pains subsided after I took the medications,"* she recalled.

However, just about a year later, Patience suddenly felt a familiar pain in her right leg. *"The pains suddenly resurfaced,"* she says. With this new development, her husband decided to take her to an orthopaedic hospital, with hopes that they would solve the problem there once and for all.

After Patience was examined and x-rayed, the report that came was beyond their worst imagination. The doctors informed them that she had a disorder in her lumbar spine, and from her medical history, it was clearly due to the fall she had the year before.

In an attempt to decisively correct the problem, her right leg was placed in traction and she had to be placed on medications of thirty tablets and several injections each day. While on medication, Patience started to observe an inexplicable numbness all over her body. It was not until her leg was removed from the traction that the gravity of her situation came to the fore.

Patience could no longer stand, walk or even sit. She had become totally bedridden. The doctors tried everything they knew to salvage the situation, but their efforts proved abortive as her condition failed to improve. Finally, when they had done all they could, they gave her husband the option to discharge her.

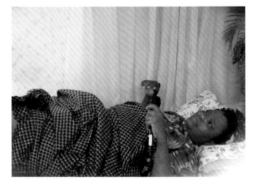

Nothing was the same again for Patience. *"I couldn't move or walk or sit upright. My backbone felt stiff,"* she said. Her condition was so dreadful, her husband had to get her diapers, as it was an ordeal for her to be carried to the restroom whenever she needed to relieve herself. Her cries of pain and agony filled the house every day. She was further tormented by spasms of coughing and breathlessness whenever she was touched.

Patience lay in bed day in, day out. A life that was once filled with radiance and vitality suddenly became so limited. Before long, she developed a bald patch at the back of her head as a result of the long hours she spent lying in bed. To move her around from place to place, her family fashioned a homemade stretcher from the headboard of a bed. This once vibrant wife and mother had become an invalid, and her husband and children watched helplessly as her life rapidly went down an incline.

Patience longed for the day she'd be normal again and return to the life she once knew. *"I prayed and cried to God everyday to take me back to the way I was before, to be restored to the way He created me."*

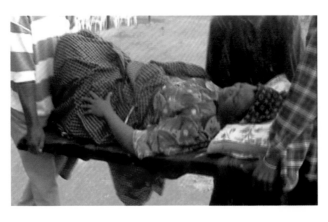

One day, while Patience lay in front of the TV, a programme caught her attention. It was a miracle program by Pastor Chris where a little boy who was on a wheelchair was miraculously healed by the power of God at the Healing School. The programme stirred up so much faith in her heart that she decided right there to attend the Healing School. She said, *"Yes, I would go to that place and receive my healing!"*

Exactly one week later, Patience was carried to the Healing School by her husband and two of her sons. She soaked up God's Word that was taught like a parched ground would soak up water. *"I knew I had come to my last point, so I grabbed the Word of God that I was taught because I had learnt that to move God into my*

Patience's husband ministering to her under the direction of the man of God.

situation, I needed faith, and faith comes from hearing the Word of God."

The day the man of God, Pastor Chris, ministered to Patience is one that would remain evergreen in her heart. Lying feebly on the homemade stretcher, she was carried to meet with him. Heartfelt prayers poured forth from the congregation when they saw the

distressing condition she was in. The man of God approached her husband, who was with her, and asked him to lay his hands on her chest and speak God's Word over her. *"He told my husband to call my name and say to me, 'You will live and not die!'"* Patience recalled.

Miraculously healed, Patience rises from the ground, giving glory to God.

Then Pastor Chris stretched his hands towards Patience. At this time the power of God was so intense that she began to vibrate and move from side to side. In that moment, the man of God tapped her on her shoulders and told her to get up. Instantly, Patience got up and stood! Suddenly, there was an expression of awareness on her face, as she knew something had happened within her.

Shouts of thanksgiving and praise erupted from the congregation as Patience stood to her feet and took some steps. It was indeed an awe-inspiring moment for everyone present. Just a few moments earlier, the woman before them was helplessly bound by an infirmity, but here she was healed and walking by the power of God!

Overwhelmed and

Mrs. Patience Agboghoroma testifying of her healing.

in awe of the miracle she had received, tears of joy ran down freely from her face as she lifted her hands in praise to God. Her husband was beside himself with joy, as he quickly went to her and embraced her. What a mighty deliverance it was! She was standing and walking normally as if she'd never suffered any paralysis!

Some months later, Patience and her husband returned to testify of her miracle and the transformation that had taken place in her life afterwards. With great energy and enthusiasm, she testified, *"I'm a living testimony of the power of the Word of God! God has completely made me whole and restored my life. With Him, all things all possible! If you've lost hope, just look at me. I'm a living proof that Jesus is real! No matter the situation, no matter how bad it is, Christ can make you whole!"* Glory to God!

Since that day, Patience has had no trace of infirmity in her body. It's been six beautiful years for her! Presently, she actively manages a poultry farm with her husband.

Walking as a Form of Exercise

Walking is one of the simplest and safest exercises you can do. It will help strengthen your bones, control your weight and is good for your heart and lungs. Walking provides the following benefits:

•It helps your heart and lungs function even better.

•It burns body fat.

•Walking raises your metabolism, so you're burning calories faster, even while you rest.

•It helps control your appetite.

•It increases your energy and reduces stress.

•Walking promotes restful sleep.

• It strengthens the bones and reduces stiffness of the joints due to inactivity

•   It improves your flexibility and posture.

•   Walking elevates mood.

Tips to help you develop an efficient walking style:

•   Hold your head straight and abdomen flat.

•   Your toes should point straight ahead and arms should swing loosely at sides.

•   Land on the heel of the foot and roll forward to drive off the ball of the foot.

•   Take long, easy strides, but don't strain for distance.

•   When walking up or down hills, or at a

very rapid pace, lean forward slightly.

- Breathe deeply (with mouth open, if that is more comfortable).

What to wear when walking:

A good pair of shoes is the only "special equipment" required by a walker. Any shoes that are comfortable, provide good support, and don't cause blisters or calluses, will do.

You could start by setting a short-term goal of walking five minutes once or twice daily. From there, you can set longer-term goals, such as walking two or three times a day for twenty minutes a session.

THE TRANSFORMING POWER OF GOD'S WORD

11

*I*magine that a certain wonder-drug with the ability to cure any kind of sickness, disease, or pain has just been produced. It's an all-round drug that can heal the body of anything. If you were barren, it would help you conceive; if you were bulimic or anorexic, it would cure the eating disorder. If you were bald, it would make your hair grow again; if you were sick with a terminal disease, it would heal it; it could do just anything!

If such a drug were possible, it would be in very high demand the world over. Even if they weren't sick, many people would like to have it, just in case anything happened. Incidentally, the Word of God is that drug! **Proverbs 4:20-22 says, "My son, attend to my words; incline thine ear unto my sayings. Let them not depart from thine eyes; keep them in the midst of thine heart. For they are life unto those that find them, and health (medicine) to all their flesh."**

THE TRANSFORMING POWER OF GOD'S WORD...

"And the disciples came, and said unto him, Why speakest thou unto them in parables? He answered and said unto them, Because it is given unto you to know the mysteries of the kingdom of heaven, but to them it is not given... Therefore speak I to them in parables: because they seeing see not; and hearing they hear not, neither do they understand" (Matthew 13:10-11,13).

In these verses of Scripture, Jesus had just rounded up teaching a large crowd in parables and His disciples came to Him and asked why He taught them that way. He explained that only the disciples had been granted revelation knowledge of the mysteries or secret truths of the Kingdom of God, which the rest of the people had not been granted. In other words, the disciples had an understanding imparted to them which the people didn't have.

Then in the fifteenth verse, the Lord said something very remarkable, *"For this people's heart is waxed gross, and their ears are dull of hearing, and their eyes they have closed; lest at any time they should see with their eyes, and hear with their ears, and should understand with their heart, and should be converted, and I should heal them."*

The word "converted" here doesn't mean a change from sinner to saint. It means a transformation of the condition of a man's life. So

Jesus was actually saying that if at any time the people have revelation knowledge imparted to their spirits, there'll be a transformation in their condition and He'll heal them. The results are automatic!

The Word of God has been programmed that way; if you see it with your eyes, hear with your ears, and understand with your heart, there'll be a transformation in your life and God's healing power will be manifested!

So the focus of Jesus' teaching here is the importance of having revelation knowledge. Now, someone may ask, "How then do I get revelation knowledge?" If you're born again and the Holy Spirit lives in you, revelation knowledge has been granted you. The Holy Spirit is the One who imparts the understanding of God's Word to every child of God. **1 Corinthians 2:12** says, ***"Now we have received, not the spirit of the world, but the spirit which is of God; that we might know the things that are freely given to us of God."***

The Holy Spirit helps you see, hear, and understand the mysteries of the Kingdom of God. If you accept and receive this revelation knowledge that He brings to you, there will be a conversion of your condition and a transformation in the circumstances of your life.

The Word of God actually functions like a step-up converter; it transforms you from one level of glory to another. It changes the circumstances of your life and brings healing to your body! When you understand this truth, you'd realize that God doesn't choose to heal one and not the other. He has said: When you see, hear and understand My Word, you'll be healed! There's no option. My healing power is in My Word!

HE SENT HIS WORD...

"Fools because of their transgression, and because of their iniquities, are afflicted. Their soul abhorreth all manner of meat; and they draw near unto the gates of death. Then they cry unto the LORD in their trouble, and he saveth them out of their distresses. He sent his word, and healed them, and delivered them from their destructions" (Psalms 107: 17-20).

It's important to note that Psalm 107:20 doesn't say, "He is sending His Word and healing them," even though the preceding verse is in the present tense. It says, "He sent His word, and healed them..." In other words, God's Word is already there. God is not making up His mind to heal anybody now. He has sent His Word; if anybody would see, hear, and understand it, he would be converted and healed.

God has already sent His Word concerning your divine healing and health. **1 Peter 2:24** says, *"Who his own self bare our sins in his own body on the tree that we, being dead to sins, should live unto righteousness: by whose stripes ye were healed."* Now, see yourself in it! Don't see yourself broken and bound by any infirmity; see yourself healed in Christ Jesus. Say to yourself, "I see now that I am the healed of Christ; I'm not what my body looks like right now! I see now that Jesus took my infirmities and bore my sicknesses. Therefore, I refuse to be sick; I have been healed in Christ Jesus!" As you do this consistently, it won't be long before God's Word will produce a miracle in your body!

Sometime ago, I heard a beautiful testimony of a lady who got terribly injured and couldn't walk anymore. She could only move with a wheelchair in that condition of excruciating pain. One day, as she sat listening to a man of God teach God's Word on television, she believed in God's healing power. She had never heard anything like that before, but as she listened, she believed the Word of God could work in her body.

From that day on, she would say, "I'm healed in the Name of Jesus!" and her doctor would reply, rather skeptically, "Yes, you are," and give her more medications. He had told her she would never be able to walk again.

One day, the lady said, "Doctor, I just found out I would be able to walk again."

"Yes, only God does such things," the doctor replied.

"Yes! God has already done it in my body," she declared.

"Who told you that?" he queried.

"There's this man on TV who's been preaching this stuff and I believe it," came her response.

"Well," the doctor said, "I don't know anything about that. Just be careful, okay?"

Sometime later, while in bed, she heard the voice of God's Spirit say, "Stand up and walk!" She got up but she fell down as she tried to walk. Then she managed to creep back to the bed.

Then the devil told her, "Never try that again!"

"Well," she said, "I heard God say, "Stand up and walk!" So she got up again, but when she tried to walk, she fell down. Then she waxed bold and said, "God told me to stand up and walk! He didn't just say 'Stand up.'" So she got up again and this time as she took a step, she declared with authority, "In the Name of Jesus, I walk!" She took another step and said the same thing. Then she took another step, and another, until she began to walk round the room, glory to God!

After that, she danced and leapt for joy until the doctor came rushing in. The moment he saw her, he broke into tears and said, "I have never seen anything like this all my life!" His skepticism flew right out the window and he believed.

This dear lady got an understanding of God's Word that caused a conversion, and she was gloriously healed by the power of God, Hallelujah!

ATTEND TO THE WORD!

"My son, attend to my words; incline thine ear unto my sayings. Let them not depart from thine eyes; keep them in the midst of thine heart. For they are life unto those that find them, and health (medicine) to all their flesh" (Proverbs 4:20-22).

The reason some people don't get the results the Word of God talks about is that they don't give enough attention to the Word. In the scripture above, notice the Bible says to "attend." The connotation here is to attend to by presenting yourself and making yourself available. The next word, "incline," is actually translated from a Hebrew word, which means "to step aside." This means that regardless of who you are and all the things you have to do, God wants you to step aside and incline your ears to His Word. You may have many things on your mind and your body may feel weak, but God is saying, *"Step aside and listen to Me, because My Words are life unto those who find them, and health to all their flesh."*

Let your life become saturated with the Word of God. The Bible says, **"When the clouds be full of rain, they empty themselves upon the earth" (Ecclesiastes 11:3).** You won't have to go up there and try to bring the rain down; the clouds will empty themselves of their own accord when they're full. Just keep taking in God's Word, and the time will come when no sickness will be able to stay in you and healing will automatically take place. You may have been trying to no avail to have children. Keep putting the Word in you, and the time will come when your body will respond and you'll have a miracle!

Confession:

As I receive the Word of God into my heart, I declare that it is working in me, producing the results it talks about in my body! The Word of God is life and health to my body. Its transforming power is changing the circumstances of my life and causing my health to spring forth, Hallelujah!

WHEN GOD STEPS IN!

12

*M*abel Sithole was only nineteen years old when she was told that she had a life-threatening disease. She had been ill for some days prior to that time, but no one considered it to be anything serious. She had a bout of fever and got unusually tired, but her parents presumed she just needed some rest from her active life as a teenager. However, when she also began to have chest pains and headaches, they knew their daughter needed medical attention.

At the hospital, tests revealed it

MABEL SITHOLE

was no ordinary chest pain. She was suffering from rheumatic heart disease, a result of permanent damage to the heart valves due to rheumatic fever. This condition is caused by a streptococcal infection which sometimes leads to inflammation of the heart and scarring of the heart valves.

These scars on the heart valves may permit leakage, causing a backward flow of blood, and may narrow the opening of the valve, restricting the amount of blood that gets through. Inflammation of the heart can persist for a long time, leaving the permanent damage that marks this disease. This condition usually produces cardiac problems such as constant fatigue, lack of stamina, chest pain, irregular pulse, shortness of breath, and fainting spells. Mabel would suffer from these symptoms and more for the next two years.

The young lady was placed on a host of medications and injections, but they only provided temporary relief as she constantly felt weak and out of strength. She suffered terrible headaches and dizziness, which affected her sight when they became intense. Her mornings were the most difficult; she recalled, "*When I woke up in the mornings, my legs would become swollen and my joints painful, and I wouldn't be able lift my legs up to walk.*"

An undergraduate student of Information Technology, Mabel was unable to keep up with her studies, as she was frequently out of school. "It always took me a long time to get ready for school because of the pains in my legs. So, sometimes, I couldn't even go." Eventually,

Mabel's health deteriorated so badly, she became fully incapacitated and had to stay in bed every day.

Scared for her life, her parents spent huge sums of money on medications and treatments, but the results were the same; they gave no lasting relief. Pandemonium broke out in their home when Mabel's two younger sisters also fell ill with the same disease. Her parents were perplexed because there was no history of rheumatic fever in either of their families and they had never had it themselves. So they couldn't understand why all their children would suffer the same disease at the same time.

Before long, the situation began to take its toll on them. Her father began to suffer from gastric ulcer while her mother suffered from arthritis. With the health of the entire family failing, Mabel's mother had to resign from her job to tend fully to her husband and kids.

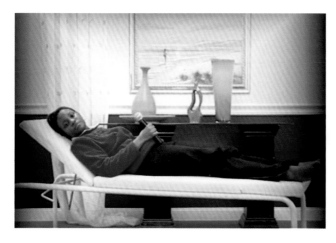

When the Sitholes heard about the Healing School, light shone in their dark world. *"It was as though God came and knocked on the door of our home when we needed Him the most,"* Mabel's mother recalled. They believed it was God reaching out to them to restore their lives.

At the Healing School, when they saw several others just like them trusting God for healing, they were encouraged in their spirits. Their faith to be healed rose to a crescendo at this time, having learned so much of God's Word on healing.

When Pastor Chris entered the hall and approached Mabel where she lay, her mother explained to him that she had two other children afflicted with the same condition. Turning to Mabel, he said he would impart the healing anointing to her, and when she returned home, she should in turn minister to her siblings.

Then the man of God stretched forth his hand over Mabel, transferring the healing anointing into her body. He placed his hand across her nostrils and instructed her to inhale deep breaths. The power of God was so intense that Mabel wept uncontrollably.

Mabel receiveing her healing as Pastor Chris ministers to her.

At that moment, the man of God declared, "*It's all over!*" and then took her by the hand and helped her to her feet. A broad, radiant smile broke on Mabel's face, and with her newfound strength she took some steps forward with the man of God!

Then the man of God blew on her, perfecting her healing and restoring her life completely. She fell to the floor under the power of the Holy Spirit. When Mabel got up, the joy on her face and the glow she radiated said it all. She had been healed completely by the power of God! Demonstrating her healing, Mabel took off across the hall with her hands lifted in praise to God!

But God wasn't through yet; Pastor Chris then ministered to her mother and she was also gloriously healed of the arthritis she had suffered! It was a beautiful sight to see Mabel run into her mother's ecstatic embrace afterwards. Her father, who was in the congregation, was also miraculously healed of gastric ulcer!

God still wasn't done with the Sitholes. When Mabel returned home, she prayed for her siblings, according to the man of God's instructions, and they were both gloriously healed by the power of God! *"The first thing I did when I got home was to ask my immediate younger sister to put on the jacket I wore when Pastor Chris prayed for me, and I laid my hands on the youngest girl. And they both*

A radiant Mabel testifying at the healing school

received their miracles!"

Two years later, a completely transformed Mabel returned to the

Healing School with her mother to testify of God's mighty power in their lives. *"Joy has returned to our home. We don't take injections anymore; we don't even go to the hospital anymore. Pastor Chris has given my family a life that's so precious."* Then her mother added, *"Now, we are taking God's Word to the ends of the earth!"*

Mabel has since concluded her diploma programme in Information Technology and is an active member of her local church.

Maintaining Fresh Breath

Everyone wants his or her mouth to smell nice and fresh all the time; and not having this experience, even if occasionally, can be somewhat embarrassing.

Here are a few steps to help you change bad breath and keep your mouth smelling nice and fresh all the time!

• *Brush your teeth regularly: Brush your teeth in the morning, after every meal, and before you go to bed. In addition, use dental floss.*

• *Brush your tongue and the roof of your mouth. This helps to dislodge unwanted substances, thereby keeping your mouth smelling fresh.*

• Clean and replace your toothbrush regularly

• Drink plenty of water. Keeping yourself thoroughly hydrated does two things: 1) it allows your system to flush out odours from onions, garlic, and other aromatic foods. 2) it also keeps your mouth moist and stifles the presence of unwanted substances, thereby preventing bad breath.

• Eat plenty of green leafy vegetables, because these contain the plant pigment chlorophyll, a natural breath freshener. Limit your intake of refined carbohydrates, coffee, and dairy products.

• Avoid caffeine: caffeine is a diuretic and can cause your mouth to become dry. A dry mouth usually doesn't smell fresh.

• *Avoid certain foods: if you don't want to smell of certain foods, then avoid eating them. Garlic, however, is good for the body, so even if you take it in large quantities, ensure proper oral hygiene afterwards.*

• *Dental care: see a dentist twice a year to have your teeth cleaned.*

• *Do not eat foods with excessive proteins and fats. If you do, make sure you remove all particles from your mouth.*

ANYTHING IS POSSIBLE!

13

"And Jesus rebuked the devil; and he departed out of him: and the child was cured from that very hour. Then came the disciples to Jesus apart, and said, Why could not we cast him out? And Jesus said unto them, Because of your unbelief: for verily I say unto you, If ye have faith as a grain of mustard seed, ye shall say unto this mountain, Remove hence to yonder place; and it shall remove; and nothing shall be impossible unto you" (Matthew 17:18-20).

"IF YE HAVE FAITH..."

Sometimes when Christians find themselves in difficult situations and they study or hear that anything is possible in Christ, they ask, "Why then did I lose the baby?" or "Why didn't our brother make it? We prayed for him and he still died. We tried everything!"

In Matthew 17:14-16, the disciples of Jesus found themselves in this kind of situation. A man had brought his son, who was oppressed by a devil, to them so they could cast the devil out. They tried everything they knew to cast out the devil, but all their efforts were to no avail. When Jesus came and met them in that situation, He cast the devil out of the boy and he was cured from that very hour (Matthew 17:18).

The disciples were stunned and they asked Jesus privately, "Why couldn't we cast him out?" Jesus didn't do anything they weren't familiar with. Otherwise, they would have said, "Oh! Master, we see now where we missed it." But they didn't say that. They were surprised because they did what He did and said what He said, but the devil didn't come out. So they asked Him, "Why couldn't we do it?"

Jesus' response is both remarkable and instructive! He told them, ***"Because of your unbelief..." (Matthew 17:20)***. Very simple but profound words! He let them know it didn't work because of their unbelief. Imagine how the disciples must have felt; they had been with Jesus for a long time, yet He told them they couldn't cast out the devil because of their unbelief.

Then the Lord said, ***"If ye have faith as a grain of mustard seed, ye shall say unto this mountain, Remove hence to yonder place; and it shall remove; and nothing shall be impossible unto you" (Matthew 17:20).*** In other words, with faith anything is possible. If it didn't work, you weren't in faith, because faith always works! Unbelief on the other hand, short-circuits the power of God.

Faith always works! Settle this truth in your heart for all time. 1 Corinthians 13:13 says, *"And now abideth faith, hope, love, these three; but the greatest of these is love."* This means that these three—faith, hope, and love—do not fade or fail; they are stable and they remain. After everything else fails, they abide. So if your faith failed, then it wasn't faith, for faith never fails; it always produces results!

The reason that situation didn't change is your unbelief. You may say, "I know I had faith." Well, Jesus said, *"If you have faith...nothing shall be impossible unto you."* Don't come back and say it didn't work. That means you're telling Jesus, *"Lord, you're not exactly right. I said what you said to say and it didn't work."*

The problem with a lot of people is that they're waiting to see a physical manifestation before they believe it worked. Jesus didn't say when you say to the mountain "remove," then watch and see it go. He said when you ask it to go, it will go. So once you make the command, begin to act as though it has gone, because it has!

It's important to understand that everything God made has intelligence. In the Old Testament, Moses proved this when he spoke to the ground and it parted wide open (Numbers 16:31-32). Joshua proved it when he spoke to the sun and moon, and they stood still (Joshua 10:12-13); Elisha proved it when he spoke to River Jordan and it parted (2 Kings 2:14); and Ezekiel proved it when he spoke to dry bones and they became a mighty army (Ezekiel 37:4-10).

Over in the New Testament, Jesus proved it too. He spoke to wind, water, bread, trees and fish, and they responded to the Word of His command. In the same way, your body has intelligence, so talk to it and it will respond!

Another important thing to notice in this scripture is that Jesus didn't say, **"If you have faith, you shall fight the mountain, or shout long enough for the devil to hear you, or beg God to take the mountain out."** No, He said, **"If you have faith, you shall SAY unto this mountain..."** In other words, if you have faith as a grain of mustard seed, you shall say to that cancer, "Go from my body" and it shall go! You'll speak to that growth, and it'll pass out of your body! You'll speak to that migraine headache, and it'll leave, and nothing shall be impossible unto you. Glory to God!

A WHOLESOME TONGUE

In Proverbs 15:4, the Bible says, **"A <u>wholesome</u> tongue is a tree of life: but perverseness therein is a <u>breach</u> in the spirit."**

The word "wholesome" used here is translated from the Hebrew word "marpê," which means "healing," "medicine," or "curative." The word "breach" is from another Hebrew word "sheber," which means "to ruin, wound, deform, or cause destruction."

So this scripture could be read thus: *"A healing tongue is a tree of life: but perverseness therein causes destruction in the spirit."* A healing tongue gives life, but a perverse tongue deforms, wounds, or causes destruction in the spirit. Another word for perverseness is "contrariness." In other words, when the tongue speaks contrary words, it causes destruction in the spirit.

Whenever you speak words contrary to God's Word concerning your life, you cause destruction in the spirit, and it's only a matter of time before the ruin shows up in the physical realm. It may come as an infection or a growth, and you may wonder, *How did this get here?* It was your tongue.

Proverbs 18:21 says, **"Death and life are in the power of the tongue."** Whether you live or die is dependent on the words you say. If someone keeps declaring, "This sickness will kill me," no matter how many doctors try to help him, he'll never get well. Why? He's signed his death into law with his own words!

James 3:4-5 also tells us something very instructive about the tongue: ***"Behold also the ships, which though they be so great, and are driven of fierce winds, yet are they turned about with a very small helm, whithersoever the governor listeth. Even so the tongue is a little member, and boasteth great things. Behold, how great a matter a little fire kindleth!"***

Your tongue is that small helm and you're the captain. If your life is headed for the rocks, and it looks like everything is getting darker, God is saying, "Use your tongue to change the direction," because you can!

Jesus said, *"If ye have faith as a grain of mustard seed, ye shall SAY unto this mountain, Remove hence to yonder place; and it shall remove; and nothing shall be impossible unto you"* (Matthew 17:20).

If a problem shows up in your body, speak faith-filled words to it! Don't speak contrary words; instead declare God's Word of healing and divine health in Christ Jesus. Jesus said, *"...ye shall SAY...and nothing shall be impossible unto you."* When you speak words of faith, anything is possible!

GUARD YOUR HEART!

Proverbs 4:23 says, *"Keep thy heart with all diligence; for out of it are the issues of life."* The Amplified Translation says, *"Keep {and} guard your heart with all vigilance {and} above all that you guard, for out of it flow the springs of life."* Don't let just anything come in; only accept the Word of God.

This is vital because you can't give what you don't have. If you don't have the Word of God in you, you can't speak it forth. **Proverbs 4:20-22** says, *"My son, attend to my words; incline thine ear unto my sayings. Let them not depart from thine eyes; keep them in the midst of thine heart. For they are life unto those that find them, and health to all their flesh."*

Let the Word of God fill your meditations. The result would be that your words will become consistent with what God's Word says. The truth is, you can't meditate on the Word of God for long enough without it changing the way you talk. It will fill your heart with faith and put away contrariness from your tongue. Jesus said, ***"If ye have faith as a grain of mustard seed, ye shall say unto this mountain, Remove hence to yonder place; and it shall remove; and nothing shall be impossible unto you"*** (Matthew 17:20).

Confession:

Nothing is impossible to me. Therefore, I take responsibility for the direction of my life. My tongue is wholesome and it is a tree of life; I speak the right words and channel my life in the right direction in the Name of Jesus. Amen.

The man of God,
Pastor Chris, at
the Healing School

Ministers and visitors from different parts of the world arrive at the Healing School of Christ Embassy to witness and experience the power of God.

Visitors from Romania

Visitors from South Africa

Visitors from Finland

A delegation from Canada

South Korean ministers attending a special meeting at the Healing School pray earnestly as they prepare to hear the Word

Visiting ministers listen as Pastor Chris teaches God's Word at the Healing School

A delegation of South Korean ministers listen with enthusiasm as Pastor Chris shares the Word during a special meeting at the Healing School.

Ministers take notes while attending a
class at the Healing School

A group of ministers from Finland witness the power of
God at a healing service

The congregation enjoys one of the many rapturous moments
during a healing service

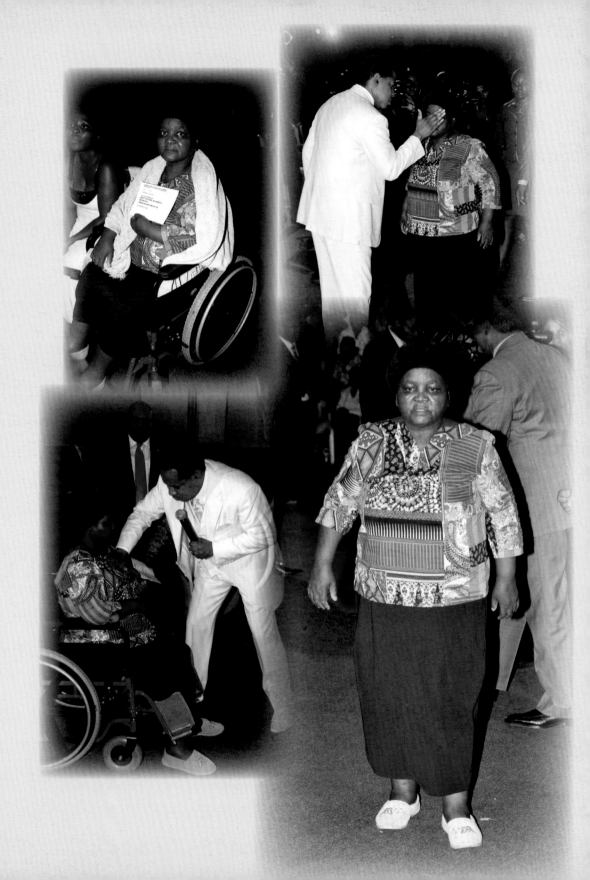

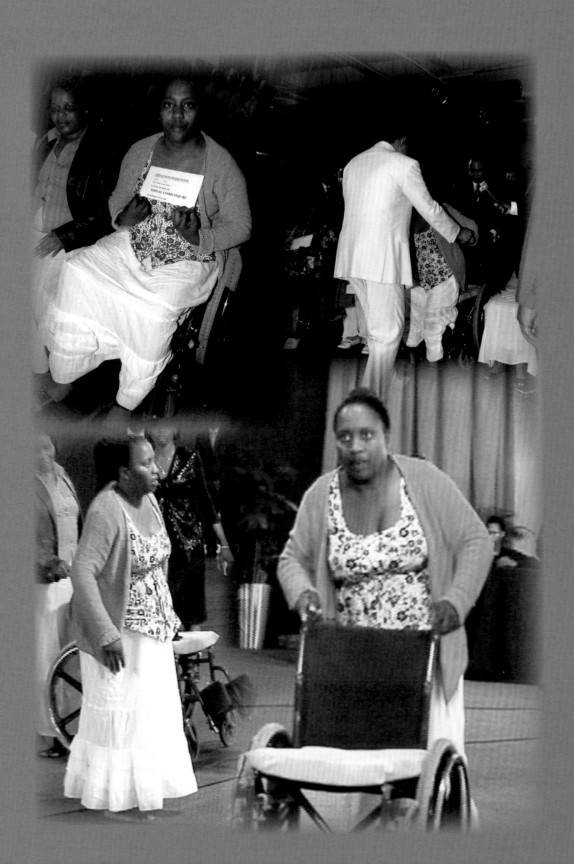

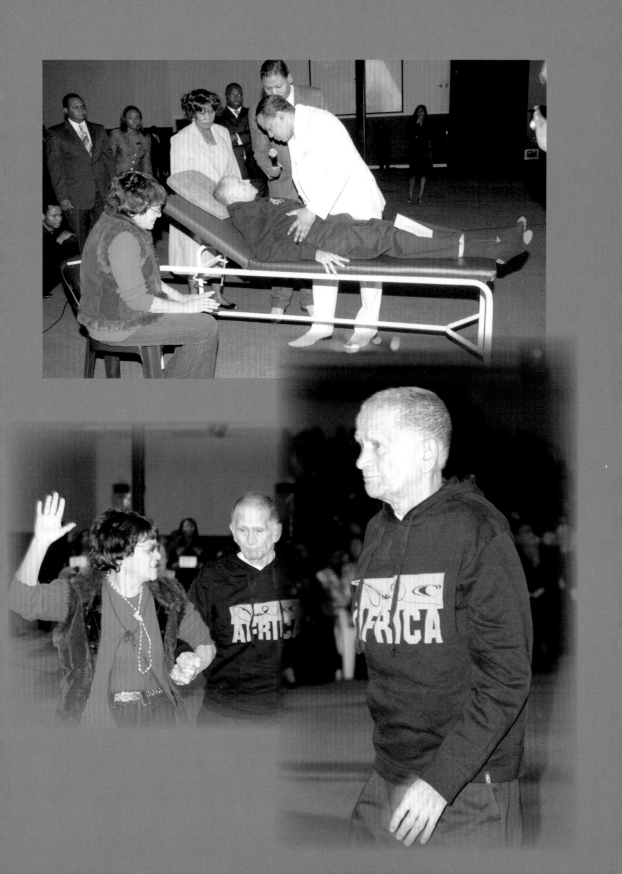

GOD HONOURS FAITH!

14

*I*t was getting close to the end of the year again, and Melania Napa'a knew what to expect. It was as sure as dawn that it would come. Since she was four, she had suffered from a condition that had defied every treatment that had been offered. Now thirteen, the teenager had mastered its timing. *"It always came like an attack towards the end of the year, and it would stay for at least one month,"* she recounted.

All through her growing years, Melania had suffered pains and swelling in her joints. When the pains came, they'd plague her for about one month,

MELANIA NAPA'A

during which her joints would swell and hurt terribly. The doctors had never really been able to diagnose the problem. Always, every doctor she was taken to had a different diagnosis. *"Since I was four, I've been in and out of hospitals, and the doctors always changed what they told me I had,"* Melania recalled.

For many years, she was treated in a Children's Hospital for recurrent joint pains. However, she never got well, as the treatments only provided temporary relief. *"There was nothing they did that helped; the pains always came back."*

By the time Melania was eight, the pains had become more recurrent and severe. *"The pains came mostly in my hips, knees, ankles and wrists. And when they came, my legs would get stiff and cramped up, and I couldn't bend them. My ankles also became swollen and very painful. My muscles would tighten and I would be unable to eat for days."* Occasionally, the pains would get so severe that Melania would have lesions over her joints.

For years, her condition confounded her doctors and they eventually arranged for her to be transferred to a specialist hospital. After extensive tests, she was diagnosed to have "recurrent arthralgia and possible arthritis." They gave her potent painkillers and suggested different types of exercises for her to do, but these also gave no lasting relief. *"The pains would go and then come back worse,"* Melania recollected.

She was scheduled to visit different types of physiotherapists and psychologists, with hopes that they would help. Nothing changed; instead, her condition got worse. Desperate for a lasting solution, her parents took her frequently to herbal homes, where they'd massage her body, but that didn't do much for her either.

Over time, Melania observed that the pains came mostly towards the end of the year. During those times, she'd suffer excruciating pains and have great difficulty walking. At such times, she'd have to be admitted into the hospital. *"I was normally in the hospital for two to three weeks, and sometimes a month. I would be unable to move my left hip down to my toes,"* she recalled.

As a young girl in grade school, this situation unavoidably affected her studies as she always had to be absent from school for long periods. *"It was really difficult for me because I always missed school and fell behind in my studies."*

More frustrating for Melania was that sometimes the pains got so bad that she had to resort to using a walking-aid. *"Sometimes, I had to be on crutches for a week or two, or sometimes three weeks. And whenever I got off them, my friends always stopped me from doing many things, saying that I might get hurt. They always reminded me about my leg, and sometimes I felt mocked."*

With time, Melania began to suffer wrenching pains in her shoulders and spasms of pain in her fingers and elbows. Terrified of their daughter's deteriorating health, Melania's parents had her transferred to another specialist hospital.

In this hospital, after further tests, the diagnosis was completely different. "*I was told by the doctors that I had hyper-mobility syndrome.*" The specialist stated clearly in her medical report: "*Episodic joint and limb pains secondary to joint hyper-mobility syndrome, which is causing damage to her joints, resulting in her ongoing episodes of pain in her hip and thigh.*"

For Melania, this report was more than she could bear. Almost all her life, she had been suffering from a condition that no one seemed to have answers to, and she desperately wanted to enjoy a normal life. "*Everything became so confusing for me. I couldn't understand why the pains always came and there was nothing that could be done. The doctors kept saying different things all the time and I never got answers. I really felt sad because there were so many things I wanted to do, which I couldn't do. I love sports, but most times I couldn't play through a whole game or play at all because I didn't want to have pains or cramps.*"

With the pains becoming more recurrent and severe, Melania found it increasingly difficult to do simple things. "*It was just hard, knowing that I wanted to do something but I couldn't, especially when I needed to get to the bathroom and I couldn't because of the pains. I couldn't sleep on my left side or bend forward or even backwards. It was always painful.*"

A few months to Melania's fourteenth birthday, she had an experience that would start the transformation that she was soon to have. "*Some Pastors came to our Church and invited everyone who needed healing to the Healing School in South Africa. I knew in my heart that this was the only way I could be healed.*"

That day marked a new beginning in the young girl's life as she not only decided to attend the Healing School, but also gave her heart to the Lord. *"I was born again that day and decided to stop the medications which hadn't made any difference for so long."*

The next session of the Healing School was scheduled to hold in a couple of months in Johannesburg, South Africa. It was a journey of over twenty-five hours from her home in Auckland, New Zealand, but she remembers how determined she was to make it, *"I knew for sure that I would go."* In spite of her pains, her hopes had soared.

Pastor Chris blows the healing anointing on Melania.

When Melania arrived at the Healing School, she had only one prayer: *"I want God to heal me from all these pains; to take them away from me and never let them come back into my life, because I know that nothing is impossible for Him and all things are possible."*

With faith in her heart, Melania stood on the healing line with many others who also had come trusting God for a miracle. She watched with rising anticipation as the man of God, Pastor Chris, ministered with compassion to each person. When her turn came, he stood before her and laid his hands on her shoulders. Melania raised her hands to heaven and her eyes glistened with tears as the man of God continued to minister to her.

Suddenly, Pastor Chris declared, "*Loose!*" and blew on her. At that moment, Melania fell back on the ground and remained there for a few minutes. "*I didn't know when I fell!*" she said. But God was doing what no doctor, therapist or medication could do for her!

When Melania got up, she knew more than anything that she had been healed. Through tears of joy, she shouted, "*Thank You Jesus!*" and bounded across the hall! It was amazing; God had turned her life around within moments and filled her heart with rejoicing!

Melania overwhelmed by her healing miracle and the instant transformation in her body

Reliving her awesome experience the next day before many others who had also been healed, she said, "*When Pastor Chris prayed for me, he imparted an anointing to me. It was such an amazing experience; I'll never forget it. It's beyond what words can explain! Last night, I slept on my left side the whole night! It was such a blessing because I could never have done that otherwise!"*

Demonstrating her healing and laughing happily the whole time, she continued to testify, *"It's a miracle! Now I can bend forward and backwards. I can move my shoulders; it's not painful anymore! The pain spasms are not there anymore! My joints are not painful anymore! If someone were to throw me a net ball now, I could play a whole game right through and wouldn't have to worry about stopping! It's just so amazing! No more pains; no more tears; I'm free! Thank you Pastor Chris for abiding in your calling. I don't know how to thank you enough; my life has been changed completely!"*

One year later, Melania is a picture of divine health and the beauty of God. She is actively involved in sports and participates freely in activities with her peers. She continues to be grateful to God for the beautiful life He made possible for her to enjoy!

Jesus said, **"If ye have faith as a grain of mustard seed...nothing shall be impossible unto you"** (Matthew 17:20).

Living Stress-Free

Living a stress-free life is one sure way of living a healthy and happy life. Stress may be considered as any physical, chemical, or emotional factor that causes bodily or mental unrest. Stress comes in various forms and affects persons of all ages and all walks of life.

Essential tips for living a stress-free life

• *Get enough sleep:*
Living a stress-free life starts with getting adequate sleep. Sleep gives your body metabolism time to rebalance, and to repair itself. It also allows your mind to rest.

• *Eat healthy:*
Eating nutritious, well-balanced meals keeps your body functioning in a positive mode. Fruits and vegetables contain antioxidants which are great stress-busters.

- *Exercise:*

Regular exercise literally washes stress hormones out of your body and releases positive hormones which soothe the mind and body.

- *Allot time for family, friends, and leisure:*

Leisure time is necessary to recharge your life. Spending time with your family and friends gives you the opportunity to relax, express yourself and regain perspective.

- *Set your goals and priorities right:*

Scheduling your day will help you cut down on activities that are not important. Always make a scale of preference of your tasks and focus on the high priority items.

Remember, living a stress-free life is all about choice.

YOU CAN CHANGE IT!

15

"And one of the multitude answered and said, Master, I have brought unto thee my son, which hath a dumb spirit; And wheresoever he taketh him, he teareth him: and he foameth, and gnasheth with his teeth, and pineth away: and I spake to thy disciples that they should cast him out; and they could not. He answereth him, and saith, O faithless generation, how long shall I be with you? how long shall I suffer you? bring him unto me. And they brought him unto him: and when he saw him, straightway the spirit tare him; and he fell on the ground, and wallowed foaming. And he asked his father, How long is it ago since this came unto him? And he said, Of a child. And ofttimes it hath cast him into the fire, and into the waters, to destroy him: but if thou canst do any thing, have compassion on us, and help *us. Jesus said unto him, If thou canst believe, all things are possible to him that believeth. And straightway the father of the child cried out, and said with tears, Lord, I believe; help thou mine unbelief. When Jesus saw that the people came running together, he rebuked the foul spirit, saying unto him, Thou dumb and deaf spirit, I charge thee, come out of him, and enter no more into him. And the spirit cried, and rent him sore, and came out of him: and he was as one dead; insomuch that many said, He is dead. But Jesus took him by the hand, and lifted him up; and he arose" (Mark 9:17-27).*

This remarkable account in the scriptures tells the story of a father who was desperate for his son's healing. His little boy had been afflicted by a deaf and dumb spirit; several times, he would suffer convulsions and the evil spirit would cast him into fire and into water in order to destroy him.

This was a complicated case, because not only did the child suffer convulsions, his condition was caused by a deaf and dumb spirit. This meant the boy was either deaf and dumb or would go deaf and dumb every time the evil spirit took over him.

The Bible also tells us he had suffered from the condition since he was a child. Imagine the emotional turmoil the boy's father and his family must have gone through until they heard about Jesus.

The man went to Jesus' disciples, but they couldn't cast the devil out. Then he met Jesus and cried out to Him, ***"...if thou canst do anything, have compassion on us, and help us" (Mark 9:22).***

Now, it's very important that you notice Jesus' response. He said, *"If thou canst believe, all things are possible to him that believeth."* The Master turned the whole thing around and said, *"The power of God can do anything, so it's not a question of what I can do; it's what you can believe."*

The man probably saw Jesus as a good miracle-worker, and that's why he spoke the way he did. That's the way some people think today, and it's wrong. They go to a minister and say, "If you can do anything, please help me." Understand that it's not what the minister can do. The question is how much can you believe?

Maybe there's a condition in your body right now and you're saying, "Oh! I wish somebody will pray for me." No, Jesus said, ***"If thou canst believe, all things are possible to him that believeth" (Mark 9:22).*** You can change that situation. It's a question of how much you can believe and what your faith can receive.

Understand that if your situation is going to change, it's going to be by your faith. It's not another person's faith or the minister's faith, but your faith that will change that situation. Jesus didn't say, *"If thou canst believe, all things are possible to God."* It says all things are possible to YOU when you believe. No matter what you're going through today, you can change it if you can believe.

FAITH IS THE VICTORY!

"For whatsoever is born of God overcometh the world: and this is the victory that overcometh the world, even our faith" (1 John 5:4).

The lack of understanding of this truth is the reason why, sometimes, when people face difficulties in their lives, they pray, "I know my God is going to do it; I know He will not fail me." Even though that sounds wonderful, it's wrong and it will not work. It's not God's responsibility to effect the change you desire; it's your responsibility.

I would to God that all of God's children would understand that Christianity is not a life that we live with the expectation that God will help us out. God has already done everything necessary for you to live a healthy, prosperous, joyful, and fulfilled life. What you need is the application of your faith.

In Matthew 17:20, Jesus said, *"...for verily I say unto you, If ye have faith as a grain of mustard seed, ye shall say unto this mountain, Remove hence to yonder place; and it shall remove; and nothing shall be impossible unto you."*

A mustard seed is a very small seed, yet Jesus said if you have faith as small as that seed, you would tell a mountain to move and it would, and nothing shall be impossible unto you. In other words, with the smallest amount of faith, you can have mighty miracles, if you would put it to work.

Faith is the substance of things hoped for, the evidence of things not seen (Hebrews 11:1). It is the confident assurance that what you have hoped for is there, and the conviction of the reality of things that you don't see.

Now, Jesus said, "*If ye have faith as a grain of mustard seed...nothing shall be impossible unto you.*" This means that with faith, you can change anything! Your faith is the victory!

If there's something in your body that you don't like, don't stay with it; change it! And you do this by voicing and acting your faith. Get to God's Word that tells you of your divine health and healing in Christ Jesus, and then voice it and act that way.

What is that mountain of infirmity that has weighed you down for so long? Don't cry to God; use your faith to remove it! When you do this, you can be sure there would be a change! Even when it seems like nothing happened, keep acting your faith; it's only a matter of time before the change will be evident for all to see, because faith always works!

Confession:

My faith is the victory that overcomes every challenge to my health. I believe God's Word that says I was healed by the stripes of Jesus. Therefore, my health shines forth today and every day in Jesus' Name, Amen.

16

PREVAILING FAITH!

DANIELLA DU TOIT

Her hazel eyes spoke of deep-rooted sadness. Daniella Du Toit was only twenty-one years old, yet she had suffered a pain many women dread for a lifetime.

From as early as she could remember, Daniella had always wanted to have children. Little wonder at the indescribable joy she felt when she found she was pregnant three months after her wedding to Cornelius Johannes, whom everyone fondly called "CJ." They had their home in Pretoria, South Africa, and like most young couples, they were overjoyed with expectancy.

For Daniella, every day was as a fleeting moment in time, as she anticipated the day she would hold her newborn baby in her arms. Those happy days passed quickly, and before she knew it, she was six-and-a half months pregnant. With barely ten weeks to go, she found herself counting the days. Little did she know that she would soon have the most traumatic experience of her life.

Daniella never saw it coming. She was at home one morning when she suddenly felt her baby become lifeless within her. She felt a pressing urge to relieve herself, and when she did, her baby passed out lifeless from her body. It was a premature stillbirth.

"When it happened, I was shocked; I just couldn't believe it. I called my husband and just started crying, and told him what had just happened. He also found it hard to believe," Daniella recalled.

At the hospital, the doctors conducted an ultrasound test and were shocked at what they found. Daniella's womb was split into two with a dividing wall in the middle. *"There's a strange partition in your uterus, and it's unlikely that you could ever carry a baby to full term,"* came the doctors' stunning verdict. To clarify their diagnosis, they went on to explain, *"When the foetus gets to its twelfth week, it would become increasingly difficult for it to receive nourishment from your bloodstream due to the restricted space caused by the partition. It's impossible for a growing*

Medical Report:

Patient: Nella du Toit

Date of Birth: 19/08/1987

Social history: No smoking. No alcohol use. Healthy appearance. Normal BMI. Married for 13 months.

Current medical status:
8 weeks pregnant on the 19th of March, 2008.
Current pregnancy high risk: On progesterone
Previous miscarriage at 20 weeks gestation. Patient has anatomical defect of the uterus. There is one cervical os, but two uteri'. Previous pregnancy probably attached to the septal wall and with increase in gestation and fetal demand from the placenta there was probably a nutritional deficit to the fetus.
Future surgical removal of septum would not necessarily give desired result due to risk of damage to endometrium and further functioning of uterus during pregnancy.

Other: Spinal anatomical defect – Spina bifida occulta.
No neurological fallout.

Cardiovascular and Respiratory system no abnormality.
No CNS defects.

Current medicine use: Progesterone, Folic acid and Iron supplements.

Previous surgery: Tonsillectomy Dental surgery

No previous hospitalization or treatment for chronic disease.

Ellenore Meyer
MBChb (Tuks)

foetus to survive in such a condition."

Any hopes that Daniella had for a solution were quelled when the doctors told her they couldn't guarantee that an operation would help. In fact, they told her point-blank that an operation was a risk because vital tissues in her womb could be damaged in the process.

More candidly, it was stated categorically in her medical report: "...future surgical removal of septum would not necessarily give desired result due to risk of damage of endometrium and further functioning of the uterus during pregnancy."

Daniella was so depressed; she felt completely at a loss for what to do. *"I was sad and cried a lot; I didn't have any hope for the circumstances."* She sought medical advice from other doctors but their responses were all the same: there was nothing they could do to help her. Some others added that it was dangerous for her to even consider getting pregnant again.

Against all odds, a few months afterwards, Daniella got pregnant again. However, with the doctor's report at the fore of her mind, her joy was mingled with fear. Within a few weeks, just as the doctors predicted, she began to experience excruciating abdominal pains.

At the hospital, her doctor simply told her that there was nothing that could be done. *"I went to the doctor and she told me there's nothing that could make my condition better. I was very disappointed; I just started crying. I knew I was about to lose my baby again,"* Daniella recalled.

Raised in a Christian home, Daniella decided to pray. At this time, she knew that if she was going to have the baby, it would be by the power of God alone. *"I was sad and depressed every day, not knowing what was going to happen to my baby. So I prayed for an answer."*

It was during this period that a family member told Daniella about an ongoing Healing School session in Johannesburg. Daniella had heard about the Healing School before from her sister and had also watched a few episodes of **"Enter the Healing School with Pastor Chris"** on TV.

"I had heard amazing testimonies about the Healing School, and how

you could get healed there of any sickness or disease or problem. So when I heard that there was just one service left, I immediately decided to go to the Healing School to get healed."

Approximately one hour's drive from her home in Pretoria, Daniella made the journey to the Healing School, filled with great expectations. The moment she got there, she knew she wasn't going to leave the same way. *"From the moment I walked into the Healing School building, I felt a touch from God; I just knew that I was going to get healed."*

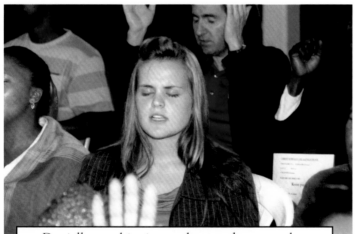

Daniella worshipping as she eagerly expects her miracle during a healing service with Pastor Chris

By this time, Daniella was ten weeks pregnant, and as she received the Word of God that she was taught, her faith grew and she could feel a transformation take place within her. *"My whole life was just changed,"* she said.

At the healing service, Daniella's heart bubbled with expectation. *"I had a very big expectation; I just knew I was going to get healed."* At this time, Daniella's faith had grown so much, and her unborn child had become real to her. *"I began to imagine how my baby would be when he was born and what people would say about my miracle baby!"* she said.

Just then, the man of God, Pastor Chris, walked into the hall and began to minister to all who were on the healing line. *"When he walked towards me, I just closed my eyes and was very expectant."* Then he stood before Daniella and laid his hands on her back. *"I felt a warm feeling go right through my whole body and then I just fell on the floor under the anointing of God."*

The moment Daniella got up, her healing was evident. Her faith had won, and she was definitely not the same again. *"As soon as I stood up from the floor, I just knew I was healed and everything was going to be fine! I didn't feel any more pain in my abdomen, and I felt so different, like a new person!"*

The transformation that had taken place in her life was even more evident when she got

The man of God ministering healing to Daniella

home that day. *"As soon as I got home, everyone just wanted to know what happened. I was so full of faith; I started planning for my baby because I knew he was going to be a perfect baby."*

True to her faith and the power of God, six and a half months later, Daniella gave birth to a healthy and beautiful baby boy, Christiaan Johannes! *"Every time people see him, they get so excited and I just can't wait to tell them the big testimony of how the Lord healed my womb and gave me this beautiful baby boy!"*

Christiaan Johannes is a living testimony of the power of faith in God. Medical science said Daniella could not carry a baby past twelve weeks, but her faith in the power of God reversed the situation and delivered to her a son!

Daniella and CJ Du Toit with their baby, Christiaan.

It's been two years since Daniella received her miracle, and she remains grateful to God for transforming her life at the Healing School. *"My experience at the Healing School changed my whole life. It made my relationship with God stronger; I'm no longer afraid of anything! Every time I face a situation that looks hard for me I just start to speak in tongues because I know nothing is impossible with God!"*

Today, Christiaan is one year and seven months,

and Daniella is pregnant with her second child!

"...With men this is impossible, but with God all things are possible!" (Matthew 19:26).

Grow Gracefully: Learn To Eat Right

Eating right is one sure way to enjoy radiant health all the time. To eat right is to eat healthy. Most people equate eating healthy to losing flavour. This cannot be more untrue. Outlined below are foods you need to cultivate a healthy diet; thus, giving your body the opportunity to grow in grace!

• *Bread, Cereal, Rice, and Pasta: Whole grain breads are low in fat; they are also high in fibre and complex carbohydrates. Choose these breads for sandwiches and as additions to meals. Avoid rich bakery foods such as donuts, sweet rolls, and muffins.*

These foods can contain more than 50% fat calories. Snacks such as angel food cake and gingersnap cookies can satisfy your curd without adding fat to your diet. Avoid fried snacks such potato and tortilla chips. Try low-fat or baked versions instead. Hot and cold cereals are also usually low in fat.

•   Vegetables and Fruits
Fruits and vegetables are naturally low in fat. They add flavour and variety to your diet. They also contain fibre, vitamins, and minerals. Margarine, butter, mayonnaise, and sour cream add fat to vegetables and fruits. Try using herbs and yoghurt as seasonings instead.

•   Meat (Beef, Pork, Veal, and Lamb) and Poultry
Baking, broiling and roasting are the healthiest ways to prepare meat and poultry.

Use either a non-stick pan or non-stick spray coating instead of oil. Trim outside fat before cooking. Trim any inside, separable fat before eating. Select low-fat, lean cuts of meats. Chicken breasts are a good choice because they are low in fat. Use domestic goose and duck occasionally because both are high in fat. Use herbs, spices, fresh vegetables, and non-fat marinades to season meat. Avoid high fat sauces and gravies.

- Fish

Poaching, steaming, baking, and broiling are the healthiest ways to prepare fish. Most sea foods are low in saturated fat. Omega-3 fatty acids are found in some fatty fish, such as salmon and cold water trout. This is good for your heart.

- Dry beans, peas, and lentils

These offer protein and fibre without the

cholesterol and fat that meats have.

• Milk, Yoghurts and Cheese
Choose skim milk, or low-fat butter milk.
Substitute evaporated skim milk for cream
in recipes for soups and sauces. Also, take
low fat cheeses instead.

Carefully choosing and eating the right
meals will enable you grow healthy and
gracefully. Why not give it a try!

WHEN THERE IS NO CHANGE AS YET

17

*W*hen you face hopeless situations, it's important to understand that God is not at all troubled by your desire for change. The truth is, He is actually watching to see you change that situation. He wants you to do something about it, and when you successfully do, He honours you for your triumph of faith.

It's your responsibility to prevail over contrary circumstances through the exercise of your faith. This is vital, because when you study God's Word, you'll find that the only fight the Christian is instructed to engage in is the good fight of faith. **1 Timothy 6:12** says, **"Fight the good fight of faith, lay hold on eternal life, whereunto thou art also called, and hast professed a good profession before many witnesses."**

There's no other fight the Christian is called to fight. The devil has been defeated. Jesus said in **Luke 10:19** says, **"Behold, I give unto** *you power to tread on serpents and scorpions, and over all the power of the enemy: and nothing shall by any means hurt you."* The world has been overcome. **John 16:33** says, ***"These things I have spoken unto you, that in me ye might have peace. In the world ye shall have tribulation: but be of good cheer; I have overcome the world."*** The flesh has been crucified. **Galatians 5:24** says, ***"And they that are Christ's have crucified the flesh with the affections and lusts."***

The only thing left is the appropriation of that which the Master has already done for us. This means holding on to what He has given you in spite of sensory evidence. This is actually what the Lord Jesus meant when He said, *"To him that overcometh..."* in several portions of Scripture in the book of Revelation (Revelation 2:7, 11, 17, 26; 3:5, 12, 21; 21:7).

See With God's Light

If you're in a condition today that you don't like, it's your responsibility to come out of it. A lot of times we think that God is going to bring us out, but the truth is, in the mind of God, you're already in the best place you could ever be. Now it's up to you to use your faith to make your life a true reflection of the Word.

1 Timothy 6:13,16 says, ***"God…Who only hath immortality, dwelling in the light which no man can approach unto; whom no man hath seen, nor can see: to whom be honour***

and power everlasting. Amen."

God dwells in the light of His Word. So when He looks at you, He sees you in the light of His Word. He doesn't see you sick, weak, or bound by any infirmity. God doesn't know that you cannot have a baby. He doesn't know that you have migraine headaches. He doesn't know you're suffering from sickle cell anaemia. You may say, "There's nothing God doesn't know." Well, you've just found out something He doesn't know.

The problem with many of God's children is that they live too much on the natural level of life. They see everything at this level. They feel something in their bodies and they conclude they're sick. They look around and they figure they can't make it. They look around and see all the difficulties of life, then they say, "Oh God, see what I'm going through!" But God is saying, "Where did you get that from? How did you get into that mess?"

Let the Word of God become the light by which you see. Then, you'd discover that condition is but a mirage; it's not real. The doctors may have said, "There's no way out, you'd never get well," but reality is what the Word of God gives you. **1 Peter 2:24** says, ***"Who his own self bare our sins in his own body on the tree, that we, being dead to sins, should live unto righteousness: by whose stripes ye were healed."***

VOICE YOUR FAITH, NOT THE PROBLEM!

In that difficult situation, it's also important to know that you've got to voice your faith. You must declare the truth of what God's Word says you have. **2 Corinthians 4:13** says, ***"We having the same spirit of faith, according as it is written, I believed, and therefore have I spoken; we also believe, and therefore speak...."*** Faith speaks!

Many times when people face difficult situations, they want to tell others about it because they think they may just die in that trouble. The truth is, you're not supposed to tell what you're going through but to tell what God's Word has done for you. Our responsibility is to testify the Word.

Get to the Word of God and discover for yourself what Christ accomplished for you, then accept it and say it! There may be a medical report that shows something has gone wrong with your physical body. Your first reaction shouldn't be to find someone to share that negative report with; you ought to declare the Word of God concerning you, which you believe in your heart. That's the fight of faith! And when you stick to the Word, you're sure to have a testimony!

STAY IN THE ENVIRONMENT OF FAITH

If you've ever seen an orange seed, I'm quite sure the one you saw didn't have leaves, branches, and fruits on it. I'm also certain it wasn't crying, "Help me, I need a stem and branches; I need roots and leaves!" When you saw it, it was just a little seed, and if you wanted to grow it, all you had to do was put it in the right environment. Everything it requires to produce a tree with roots, leaves, branches, and fruits (with many more seeds in them) is inside that little seed.

All a seed requires is to be placed in the right environment and it will grow. The environment you need for that change you desire to take place is the environment of faith. If you're outside the environment of faith, you're in trouble because that's where fear, failure, and defeat thrive. **Hebrews 11:6** says, ***"But without faith it is impossible to please him: for he that cometh to God must believe that he is, and that he is a rewarder of them that diligently seek him."***

When you function in faith, it doesn't matter what you go through, your life will be tops all the time! Even when change seems impossible, you'd know that you can only come out victorious!

Confession:

I hold on to God's Word, no matter what I see or hear. I am an overcomer and I live the overcoming life. I don't fight the devil because he has been defeated already. Instead, I walk in the consciousness of my victory in Christ Jesus. Today, I walk free of every sickness or infirmity and walk in the light of God's Word.

IT'S NEVER TOO LATE WITH GOD!

18

*I*t was early one cold September morning of 1981 in Brasov, Romania.

Lorenz Marinescu had just had his bath and was preparing to go fix a fault in the pipe organ at his Church. But as he got ready, he felt some water had been trapped in his ears when he took his bath. *"I felt some water remained in my left ear, but I didn't pay any attention,"* he recalled.

Lorenz was only out of his house a few minutes when he suddenly felt something cold

LORENZ MARINESCU

deep inside his left ear. The weather was cold, but that sudden chill was odd. As Lorenz wondered what could have caused it, he began to hear a strange buzzing noise inside the ear.

A prolific organ player in his church and actively involved in several international concerts, Lorenz became agitated. He was a music professor who knew there was a call of God upon his life to minister through music, so he couldn't imagine having any problems with his hearing. *"I was a little concerned with the situation. So I immediately sought medical help,"* he said.

At the hospital, a doctor carefully examined his ears, but found nothing wrong with them. *"He just told me everything was okay. But I insisted that there was a noise inside my left ear that only I could hear."* To calm his fears, the doctor told him to relax, and that the noise would eventually stop. *"But it never stopped,"* Lorenz said.

In search for answers, Lorenz went to another doctor, who diagnosed that the hearing nerve in his left ear had been damaged. *"He told me it was probably due to the cold I felt inside it."* The doctor went ahead to explain that due to the damage, the hearing power of his left ear had become low, and consequently, he could no longer hear high pitches.

When Lorenz asked if there was anything that could be done, the doctor simply said: *"This condition is irreversible; there's nothing any doctor can do."* Refusing to give up all hope, Lorenz travelled to other countries for a solution. But every doctor he met returned with the same verdict: *"Your hearing nerve has been damaged; there's absolutely nothing that can be done."*

Worse still, they stated further that there was no medication that could help, and that it could never be healed. *"I went to Germany and Hungary,"* Lorenz recalled, adding, *"and they told me it was all over; that no eardrops, drugs or any medication could help, because the nerve had been damaged and it couldn't be healed."*

The next twenty-seven years were difficult for Lorenz. *"The buzz in my left ear was present all the time; every sound I heard was distorted. If anyone tried to whisper something in my left ear, it was impossible for me to distinguish what was said. I always had to turn my right ear to hear properly and understand. Irrespective of how close the sound was, I couldn't hear and distinguish anything with my left ear,"* he recounted.

The simple joy of hearing everyday sounds became a thing of the past, and Lorenz longed for the day when he would hear again with his left ear. *"I couldn't even hear the ticking of my watch or use my left ear on the phone, and I really got tired of it."* Deep down inside though, Lorenz knew that one day, a solution would come from God. *"I always had the assurance God would do something about this situation. I knew that only the hand of God could take away this noise and revive my hearing nerve."*

Sometime in 1996, Lorenz watched a miracle programme by Pastor Chris on Christian TV. The programme impacted him so deeply, he never forgot it. *"I still remember the presentation of that great miracle on the programme. It was an impossible situation in the life of a relatively young woman that couldn't be solved by medical science. She was carried in on a chair by four men but she was immediately healed by the power of God at work in Pastor Chris! I was amazed as I watched her get up into an upright position all by herself from the chair and walk! I was pinned to my chair in front of the TV-set; I could hardly breathe. I was in awe of the miracle. At that moment, I realized that there was something more I needed to know about healing from God."*

However, as it often happens with protracted illnesses, Lorenz had become accustomed to his hearing defect. He managed through every day as he tried to make the most of his hearing with his right ear. *"Somehow, I got used to the buzz in the ear and I was thankful that I could hear with my right ear,"* he admitted.

In September 2007, something happened that made Lorenz decide for a miracle, and that the Healing School was the place to go. *"My father suffered a severe stroke with cerebral thrombosis. He couldn't walk and talk anymore and had to depend on others for everything. In this sad situation, I began to remember the miracles that I saw years ago on TV. Then I told my wife that the Healing School was the solution for us. She agreed with me immediately, and I began watching the Healing School videos on the Internet more intensively."*

By February 2008, Lorenz's faith had grown so strong, he began to prepare to attend the next session of the Healing School scheduled to hold in Johannesburg, South Africa, in August that year. Incidentally, at this time, his mother was suffering from a back condition and his brother from allergic rhinitis. So he decided to register them as well for the Healing School. "*We were all very expectant and filled with hope. In faith, we saw every one of us healed and coming back home with miracles,*" Lorenz recalled.

However, on the 1st of July, 2008, before they could conclude all their travel documentation, Lorenz's father passed on. But his faith remained unshaken. The next month, with great expectations for the miraculous, Lorenz, his mother, and brother flew seventeen hours from Denmark, where he lived, to the Healing School in Johannesburg, South Africa.

When Lorenz arrived at the Healing School and saw many others with impossible cases healed by the power of God, it confirmed what he already believed in his heart: the Healing School was a place of the miraculous, where the power of the Holy Ghost was mightily at work.

At the healing service, Lorenz was so full of expectations; he knew he wasn't going to leave the same. "*I was very excited and expectant in my heart. I knew that something was going to happen that would change my life forever. And it did!*"

As they prayed and worshipped God, Pastor Chris walked into the hall and began to minister to all who were on the healing line. "As I waited for the moment he'd get to me, I knew in my heart *that there would be a radical change in my life.*" Then the man of God stood before Lorenz and blew the healing anointing on him. "*Immediately, I fell down by the power of God and I felt a surge of the anointing go through me. I knew at once that I had been healed and renewed totally!"*

Moments later, Lorenz got up bubbling over with joy. *"I had never felt in my left ear what I felt that day. I could hear all the sounds around me clearly!"* he said. His joy knew no bounds when he saw his mother and brother also gloriously healed by the power of God!

A healing touch for Lorenz Marinescu

When Lorenz returned to Denmark, just as he had believed in his heart, his life was radically transformed! Not only did he continue his ministry in music, he also became a soul winner extraordinaire! Indeed, Lorenz has returned to the Healing School on several occasions, bringing many others to partake of the same anointing that transformed his life. *"I testified of my healing and the Healing School to my pastors and friends in Denmark and Romania. I came back with some of them so that they may also catch the fire; and their lives and ministries have been radically changed!"*

More touching for Lorenz is that his experience at the Healing School has transformed his walk with God. *"I have grown in faith and in the knowledge of God because of the teachings I heard at the Healing School. They have completely changed my life and walk with God. Also, the truths of the Word of God are more real to me now. Now, I take the Word of God as it is, because its truths are undeniable."*

Today, alongside his ministry as the organ player, Lorenz serves as the co-pastor in his church. He preaches the Word of God there with boldness and mighty demonstrations of the power of God.

"I've got it!" Lorenz proclaims his healing.

Caring For Your Ears

The ear is a delicate sensory mechanism that provides vital information about the outside environment to our brain. It is one of the most important parts of our body. Therefore, it is important that they are cared for and protected from harm.

Cleaning your ears:

• Use soap to clean the outer portion of your ears.

• Don't clean too often and too harshly. Many imagine that ears need vigorous and daily cleaning. However, that is not good for your ears. The internal ear canal is coated with a thin and soft skin. Vigorous and daily cleaning may damage it.

• Ear wax is usually removed on its own by the ear. However, it's important to clean out excess wax regularly.

• Never try to clean your ears with any hard thing such as hair pins, or other hard objects.

• If you have pierced ear lobes, you must clean your earrings and earlobes frequently with cleansers.

General care:

• Avoid excessive sound volumes.

• Always wear a helmet when riding a bike or bicycle.

• On a sunny day, wear a hat or apply some sunscreen on your ears.

• During winter, keep your ears covered

with a hat or headband.

• Always dry your ears after swimming and shake out excess water, especially if you feel it stuck in there.

• Don't spend too much time with a cell phone in your ears or headphones. They could damage your ears over time.

Proper ear care is important to your overall wellbeing and would prevent serious ear problems. And the truth is that it doesn't take much time or effort. You only need to do it on a regular basis.

OUR WALK OF FAITH

19

"For we walk by faith, not by sight:"(2 Corinthians 5:7).

Faith is the way of life of the Christian. Another translation of the above verse says: **"But we live by faith, not by what we see" (CEV).** This means we live by faith and not by our sensory perceptions. We regulate or conduct our lives by faith in God's Word and not by what our senses perceive. We accept whatever the Word of God says as the final authority in our lives.

FAITH IS...

In **Hebrews 11:1**, the Bible gives us the best definition of faith. It says, **"Now faith is the substance of things hoped for, the evidence (proof) of things not seen."** Faith is the proof that you have what you hoped for. You don't say, "I'm trying to 'faith' it," or "I'm trying to get it by faith," because faith means you have the proof that it's yours.

If it's true faith, you won't come back to say, "I had faith for it but it didn't work." Faith means it worked because faith is the evidence. You can't have evidence of something that doesn't exist. Faith doesn't try to get or receive something. Faith claims it has happened because it has already possessed it!

BELIEVING IS NOT FAITH...

There's a big difference between believing and faith. The journey of faith however starts with believing. Believing is a state of your spirit, based on information that you have accepted and endorsed.

Faith on the other hand is action. It is acting on what you believe. You can believe something in your heart, but until you act on it, it's not faith. Your action is what really proves your believing.

In **Romans 10:9,10** the Bible says, ***"That if thou shalt confess with thy mouth the Lord Jesus, and shalt believe in thine heart that God hath raised him from the dead, thou shalt be saved. For with the heart man believeth unto righteousness; and with the mouth confession is made unto salvation."***

You believe with your heart, but until you act your believing by confessing the Lordship of Jesus with your mouth, you will not be saved. Believing is where it starts, but to experience the reality of

God's Word, your believing must translate to faith. You've got to act on what you believe.

James, talking about this says, ***"Thou believest that there is one God; thou doest well: the devils also believe, and tremble. But wilt thou know, O vain man, that faith without works is dead?" (James 2:19-20).*** In other words, don't only believe; you've got to prove your believing with corresponding action.

Believing alone will not change anything; it will only give you a good conscience before God. It's faith— acting on God's Word—that makes the difference!

EXERCISE YOUR FAITH!

Now, the Bible shows us that every one of God's children has faith. It's not something you squeeze out and try to do. It was imparted to your spirit the day you were born again. **Romans 12:3 says, *"For I say, through the grace given unto me, to every man that is among you, not to think of himself more highly than he ought to think; but to think soberly, according as God hath dealt to every man the measure of faith."***

However, that measure of faith you've got is not enough for everything. It's got to grow! When you use your faith, the result is that it would reproduce and multiply. Also, you would have more confidence to walk by faith, because of the results you've had!

If you were taking five tablets a day for a medical condition, keep speaking the Word and acting your faith. Soon you'll notice that you'll need only two tablets a day. Then after some time, you'll discover one tablet is doing the job of five. Before long, you'll be completely off the drugs and living free of medication!

You must use the Word and fight the fight of faith. The Bible says, **"...Resist the devil and he will flee from you" (James 4:7).** That's how you grow your faith, and when you win, you'd start enjoying life without drugs and pains!

Now, you can be sure that satan will try to fight you in every way to bring the pains back to your body. However, when you feel that pain, even if all you have is a little strength at the time, speak in other tongues forcefully and rebuke the devil sharply.

Your response to circumstances and events is very important. There are folks who yell their grandfather's name or some meaningless words when they hit their leg against something. Don't do that! When something like that happens, take a hold of your leg and shout, **"Be healed!"** You may feel a lot of pain; you may even be bleeding from the impact, but speak to your leg and say, *"I declare you are every whit whole!"*

Start exercising your faith today. It won't be long before it becomes giant faith; and then you'll find yourself doing great things and living the glorious life God planned for you, Hallelujah!

Confession:

I voice my faith and declare that what God's Word says I have is mine now. As I discover what I have in Christ and say it, I'll surely have a testimony! I function in faith, and the beauty and glory of God shine through me, Hallelujah!

ELIZABETH'S STEP OF FAITH

20

*E*lizabeth Bilwane was on the threshold of her golden years when she had the car accident that changed everything. The fifty-four-year-old lady was taken to the hospital in such a terrible shape, the doctors didn't think she'd ever walk again. She had sustained severe fractures and injuries in both legs.

A closer examination however revealed that the situation was not completely impossible. The fractures were in her right knee and left ankle, and they could

ELIZABETH BILWANE

insert screw plates to hold the broken bones together until they got healed.

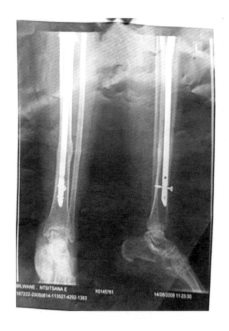

At the end of the operation, Elizabeth heaved a sigh of relief when the doctors reassured her that a short period of rest was all she needed and she'd be back on her feet in no time. She was only to return after a few months to have the screw plates removed.

Contrary to her expectations, life didn't return to normal for Elizabeth after the operation. Several months after, she still couldn't walk without difficulty. She had an obvious limp and found it too exerting to walk long distances. "*I was disappointed that the bones never got healed,*" she says.

Seven years on, and the situation kept deteriorating. Soon, she developed an infection inside her ankles where the screw plates had been

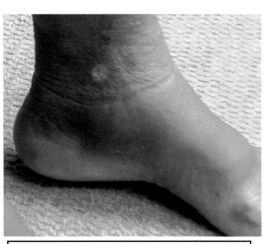

Elizabeth's ulcerated ankle swollen with pus

inserted. An operation had to be performed to contain the infection. Unfortunately, during the operation, the screw plates cut through her leg and injured her ankle. This would mark the beginning of several more months of excruciating pain for Elizabeth.

For the next ten months, no matter what was tried, the wound on her ankle never healed. It constantly dripped pus and Elizabeth had to have it cleaned regularly at the local hospital. This situation made life unbearable for Elizabeth. Recounting the ordeal, she said, *"I couldn't walk properly or run or even climb stairs. I had pains all the time. I was constantly worried that I would never walk well again and that I would have this wound for the rest of my life."*

She began attending the Orthopaedic Hospital where she could receive specialized treatment for the now chronic leg ulcer.

Sometime during this period, Elizabeth heard about the Healing School. *"I heard about the Healing School from my son. I decided to go because I wanted God to heal me and make my leg normal again. I believed He could heal me through the*

Elizabeth receiving the healing anointing as Pastor Chris ministers to her.

man of God, Pastor Chris."

At the Healing School, her faith for a miracle was stirred when she received the Word of God that she was taught. *"I had been a Christian for thirty years, but I have never heard the Word of God preached the way Pastor Chris preached it. It opened my eyes and gave me faith for a miracle."*

At the healing service, the man of God took hold of Elizabeth's hand and blew the healing anointing on her. Elizabeth was so overwhelmed by the power of God that she immediately fell down. *"When Pastor Chris prayed for me, I felt cold and dizzy and then felt the pains leave! I was so overwhelmed by the power of God!"*

Exuberant and filled with great joy, Elizabeth testified shortly after, *"I don't feel the pains anymore! I can move my legs well now! I have been healed! Thank you Pastor Chris for praying for me!"* Then without a care in the world, she jumped and raised her legs freely, demonstrating her healing for all to see! The power of God had touched her life and healed her of an infirmity that plagued her for many years, and she was overwhelmed with joy!

It was not until a few days after Elizabeth returned home from the Healing School that she realized she had also been healed of the wound. To her amazement the wound gradually closed up, and within weeks, it became completely dry! The only sign that there was ever any injury was a scar on her ankle.

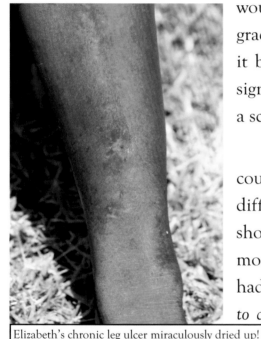

Elizabeth's chronic leg ulcer miraculously dried up!

Elizabeth also found that she could walk freely without any pains or difficulty. Returning to the hospital a short while afterwards, her doctor was most amazed when he saw the wound had completely healed. *"He told me not to come back because there was nothing wrong with me anymore, praise God!"*

Today, Elizabeth lives free from all the pains that limited her life for so many years. Every day, she's excited about her life and grateful to God for making her whole!

"If thou canst believe, all things are possible to him that

believeth!" (Mark 9:23)

Maintain Your Glow

In today's fast-paced world, often, we find ourselves enmeshed in a flurry of activities - projects to deliver at the work place, caring for the family, achieving personal goals and targets, the list is endless.

However, in the midst of all that, you must always remember that there is ONLY ONE YOU on the face of the whole earth! Therefore, you must take care of "you," so you can always be aglow!

Outlined are a few sure steps that would help you maintain your glow and keep you fresh all the time:

•   Eat right:
The state of your body is majorly a reflection

of what you eat. Aim to always include foods with high fibre, such as beans and oat meals; whole grain foods such as brown rice, brown bread and toasted wheat cereals; plenty of fresh fruits and vegetables, as well as dairy products such as pastas and breakfast cereals that are not whole grain.

• Work out:
Regular exercise will give you a youthful and radiant appearance. It also serves to strengthen your heart and lungs, thereby improving your blood circulation. Studies have also shown that physical exercise promotes better sleep and your general sense of wellbeing.

• Laugh!:
While science has not been able to fully explain it, statistics show that those who laugh more are less prone to fall ill. So take time in the day to laugh, whether or not you feel like it!

• *Have quiet times:*
Quiet times help you stay refreshed and focused. At such times, you have fellowship with God and receive guidance in your spirit on the things you do. This helps you maintain a calm and confident composure, so that you are never ruffled or perturbed.

• *Help someone in need:*
When you help people, you are enriched, not just materially, but physically too. You find that you are always filled with joy because you made a difference in someone's life. This takes depression and anxiety far from you and gives you a cheerful countenance.

Put these things to practice today, and watch yourself glow today and always!

DEMONSTRATING YOUR FAITH IN GOD

21

"And a certain woman, which had an issue of blood twelve years, And had suffered many things of many physicians, and had spent all that she had, and was nothing bettered, but rather grew worse, When she had heard of Jesus, came in the press behind, and touched his garment. For she said, If I may touch but his clothes, I shall be whole. And straightway the fountain of her blood was dried up; and she felt in her body that she was healed of that plague. And Jesus, immediately knowing in himself that virtue had gone out of him, turned him about in the press, and said, Who touched my clothes? And his disciples said unto him, Thou seest the multitude thronging thee, and sayest thou, Who touched me? And he looked round about to see her that had done this thing. But the woman fearing and trembling, knowing what was done in her, came and fell

down before him, and told him all the truth. And he said
unto her, Daughter, thy faith hath made thee whole; go in
peace, and be whole of thy plague" (Mark 5:25-34).

FAITH SPEAKS!

Mark 5:25-34 tells the story of a certain woman who had suffered a haemorrhage for twelve long years. She had been through so much trying to get well, and had spent all she had, but she didn't get any better; instead she grew worse.

In the twenty-seventh verse, the Bible says, **"When she had heard of Jesus, came in the press behind and touched His garment. For she said, if I may touch but his clothes I shall be whole."** In other words, before this woman went to Jesus, she heard about Him and learnt He was anointed with the power to heal. And she believed what she heard. Then she said, **"If I can just get close enough to touch even the hem of His garment, I shall be well."** She said it; she voiced what she believed.

In demonstrating your faith in God, it's important to understand that believing is not the end. You start with believing, but you've got to voice what you believe in your heart. That's how faith works! First, you believe, and then you speak. **2 Corinthians 4:13** says, **"We having the same spirit of faith, according as it is written, I believed, and therefore have I spoken; we also believe, and therefore speak...."**

The spirit of faith works by believing and speaking.

In this account, the woman believed in the power of God at work in Jesus Christ, and she said it. She didn't keep quiet. When faith comes alive in your heart, you can't remain quiet! You'd voice or act it out. There would be a corresponding action. A similar thought is expressed in **Matthew 12:34,** where the Bible says *"...for out of the abundance of the heart the mouth speaketh."*

FAITH ACTS!

Faith in God is demonstrated by action. Someone may be in need of healing, and then say to himself, "I know if I get into that meeting, I will be healed," but he never goes. This is the problem with many people; they talk their believing, but they don't act it. Believing must go with the corresponding action of faith; otherwise, it wouldn't produce any result.

James 2:17 says, *"Even so faith, if it hath not works, is dead, being alone."* This means that faith without corresponding action is dead. Notice, the Bible is not saying, "Faith without works is incomplete" No! It says faith without works is dead! In other words, faith without works is no faith. Faith must be accompanied by action!

In the account above, the Bible tells us that when the woman heard about Jesus, she *"...came in the press behind, and touched his garment. For she said, If I may touch but his clothes, I shall be whole"* (Mark

5:28). She heard about Jesus, and then took steps to look for Him. Interestingly, the Bible records that when she got to where Jesus was, she saw a crowd, but she *"...came in the press behind"* and touched his clothes! In her condition, she pressed her way through the crowd until she was able to reach out and touch the hem of Jesus' garment. What an effort she must have made! Then, the Bible says, *"...she felt in her body that she was healed of the plague."* The 12-year-long issue of blood stopped instantly, Hallelujah!

Now, it's important to note that Jesus didn't do anything for the woman to get the power to be healed. He was headed somewhere, and she came and touched the hem of His garment and was healed! That's the reason He didn't say to her, "My faith hath made thee whole" but "Thy faith hath made thee whole." It was her faith that made her whole. She acted on what she believed and she received a miracle!

In another account, while Jesus was teaching one day, four men brought a friend who was paralyzed. The Bible records that the crowd was so much and they couldn't get in. But these four men were undaunted; they climbed up the roof of the house, tore open a hole in it, and let down their sick friend right before Jesus (Mark 2:1-11). ***"When Jesus saw their faith, he said unto the sick of the palsy, Son, thy sins be forgiven thee...Arise, and take up thy bed, and go thy way into thine house" (Mark 2:5, 11).*** And the man got up! Hallelujah!

Now notice, the Bible says, "When Jesus saw their faith...." This means their faith was seen through their actions. They believed Jesus had the power to heal, but they didn't just stay there; they acted what they believed and they received a miracle. That's how you demonstrate your faith in God—by acting on what you believe.

Remember that God always rewards faith. When you take a step of faith, God meets you at that point and rewards you. **Hebrews 11:6** says, ***"But without faith it is impossible to please him: for he that cometh to God must believe that he is, and that he is a rewarder of them that diligently seek him."***

FAITH DOESN'T CONSIDER FEELINGS!

"Therefore I say unto you, What things soever ye desire, when ye pray, believe that ye receive them, and ye shall have them" (Mark 11:24).

A lot of times, we find people who think they have to first receive something before they can believe it. They think the only way they're going to know they're healed is when they don't feel the pain anymore. As long as they feel the pain, they think they're not yet healed. For example, someone may claim his healing and say, *"Lord, I receive my healing; I'm healed!"* but right after that he thinks, *Now that I have claimed my healing, the pain ought to be gone.* That's emphatically wrong!

In demonstrating your faith in God, it's important to understand that faith is a choice to stay in the Word. If you go by your feelings and say, "Well, I still feel the symptoms" or "If I've truly received my healing, the pains ought to have gone," it means you think receiving your healing is predicated on the absence of the pains or symptoms, and that's not what the Word says. Faith must be based on the Word of God. You accept what the Word has said, whether or not there's physical evidence, and act that way.

Hebrews 11:1 says, ***"Now faith is the substance of things hoped for, the evidence of things not seen."*** So if you say it's only when you feel something that you would accept its reality, then you're not demonstrating faith in God. In **Jonah 2:8,** the Bible says something very instructive: ***"They that observe lying vanities forsake their own mercy."*** Lying vanities are circumstances, feelings, or things that sway your focus from God's Word. They are empty and powerless in themselves but they try to dominate your mind by posing as the truth, and they thrive when you give them attention.

The Bible says those that observe lying vanities turn themselves away from God, Who offers mercy. They set aside the grace and healing that they should rightfully enjoy. Those feelings in your body are lying vanities; that doctor's report that says you've got cancer in your stomach is a lying vanity; that x-ray that shows you're almost gone is a lying vanity!

Settle in your heart today that the Word of God is true! Accept that you have whatever He says you have and you are whatever He says you are. Then go ahead and act on it with faith in your heart. For instance, **Romans 8:11** says, *"But if the Spirit of him that raised up Jesus from the dead dwelleth in you, he that raised up Christ Jesus from the dead shall give life also to your mortal bodies through his Spirit that dwelleth in you"* (ASV).

Also, **Isaiah 53:5** says, *"But he was wounded for our transgressions, he was bruised for our iniquities: the chastisement of our peace was upon him; and with his stripes we are healed."*

When you act on truths in God's Word such as these, you can rest assured that there will be a change, because God always honours faith!

Confession:

God's Word is nourishment for my spirit, refreshment for my soul and health to my body. I pay attention to God's Word and believe what it says about me. God's Word says I'm healed. I believe it with my heart and I say it with my mouth. I'm healed!

CONCLUSION

"For this purpose the Son of God was manifested, that he might destroy the works of the devil" (1 John 3:8).

Jesus successfully put an end to the works of the devil so you may live victoriously in this life. In the verse of scripture above, the Bible tells us that's why He came—to destroy the works of the devil.

Sickness and infirmity are works of the devil. If you believe in all that Jesus accomplished through His death, burial and resurrection, and confess His Lordship over your life (Romans 10:9), there's no sickness or infirmity that can have power over you. Jesus neutralized their power through His victory on the Cross over 2,000 years ago!

Colossians 2:15 says, **"And having spoiled principalities and powers, he made a shew of them openly, triumphing over them in it."** The devil has no power anymore to harm you. Jesus has stripped him of all his power and made a public spectacle of him. All he has now are "lying vanities," which he uses today to deceive many. And in **Jonah 2:8,** the Bible says, *"They that observe lying vanities forsake their own mercy."*

Refuse to let the devil rob you of your joy and happiness by inflicting your body with infirmities. He has been absolutely defeated! In **1 Peter 5:8,** the Bible says, *"Be sober; be vigilant because your adversary the devil, as a roaring lion, walketh about, seeking whom he may devour:"*

Notice, the Bible says the devil is "as a roaring lion"; he is not a roaring lion but only appears as one. So don't ever be intimidated by him. If he tries to attack you with sickness or infirmity, stand your ground on God's Word and command him, "Get out!" Remember, **1 John 5:4** says, *"...this is the victory that overcometh the world, even our faith."* Your faith in God's Word will keep you standing and drive the devil out of your territory!

When this becomes your lifestyle, your life becomes an unending stream of the miraculous and, before long, you'll be impacting your world with healing from heaven!

Confession:

I believe in the efficacy of God's Word. My faith wins all the time; it is proof-producing and brings forth testimonies. My health springs forth speedily, and I radiate God's goodness.

To contact the author, write:
Pastor Chris Oyakhilome:

UNITED KINGDOM:
Christ Embassy Int'l Office
LoveWorld Conference Centre
Cheriton High Street,
Folkestone, Kent CT19 4QS
Tel:+44(0) 1303 270 970
Fax: 01303 274 372

SOUTH AFRICA:
303 Pretoria Avenue
Cnr. Harley and Bram Fischer,
Randburg, Gauteng, South Africa.
Tel: +27 11 3260971
+27 11 3260972

NIGERIA
LoveWorld Conference Centre
51 - 53 Kudirat Abiola Way
P.O. Box 13563 Ikeja, Lagos.
Tel:+234-8023324188,
+234-8052464131, +234-1-8925724

or email:pastorchris@christembassy.org
Please include your testimony or help received from this book
when you write.
Your prayer requests are also welcome.

RHAPSODY OF REALITIES
DEVOTIONAL STUDY BIBLE

AVAILABLE IN 3 SIZES:

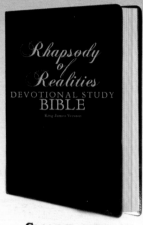

SMART SIZE

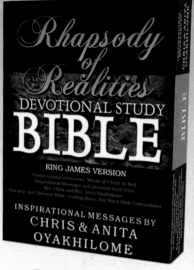

STANDARD SIZE

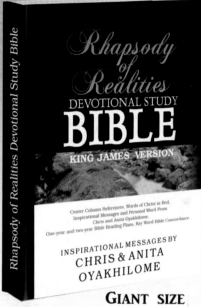

GIANT SIZE

Features

Full Color Pages of Inspirational Articles

Center Column References

Words of Christ in Red

1 Year & 2 Year Bible Reading Plans

Index to the Inspirational Articles

96 Page Concordance to the Old and New Testament

Packaging Options Include:
* Bonded Leather
* Genuine Leather
* Hard Back &
* PVC Leather

...truly your study companion for life

www.enterthehealingschool.org

Home page   Magazine   Videos   Group Visits   Community

Enter the Healing School
with Pastor Chris *Online*

Books, Bibles, Devotionals Journals, Periodicals..

- ❦ PROPHECY: UNDERSTANDING THE POWER THAT CONTROLS YOUR FUTURE
- ❦ HOW TO MAKE YOUR FAITH WORK
- ❦ PRAYING THE RIGHT WAY
- ❦ THE POWER OF TONGUES
- ❦ THE GATES OF ZION
- ❦ JOIN THIS CHARIOT
- ❦ DON'T STOP HERE!
- ❦ 7 THINGS THE HOLY SPIRIT WILL DO IN YOU
- ❦ 7 THINGS THE HOLY SPIRIT WILL DO FOR YOU
- ❦ WHEN GOD VISITS YOU
- ❦ HOW TO RECEIVE A MIRACLE AND RETAIN IT
- ❦ NOW THAT YOU ARE BORN AGAIN
- ❦ THE HOLY SPIRIT AND YOU
- ❦ NONE OF THESE DISEASES
- ❦ THE OIL AND THE MANTLE
- ❦ YOUR RIGHTS IN CHRIST
- ❦ KEEPING YOUR HEALING
- ❦ THE PROMISED LAND
- ❦ RECREATING YOUR WORLD
- ❦ RHAPSODY OF REALITIES DAILY DEVOTIONAL
- ❦ RHAPSODY OF REALITIES TOPICAL COMPENDIUM (VOL
- ❦ DON'T PACK YOUR BAGS YET!
- ❦ WISDOM FOR WOMEN
- ❦ UNENDING SPRING OF JOY

LoveWorld Publishing...

Reaching Out With The Gospel.
Building Up The Saints With Excellen
And Clarity.